Manzanilla

CHRISTOPHER FIELDEN
& JAVIER HIDALGO

Grub Street • London

Published in 2010 by
Grub Street
4 Rainham Close
London
SW11 6SS
Email: food@grubstreet.co.uk
Web: www.grubstreet.co.uk

Text copyright © Christopher Fielden &
Javier Hidalgo 2009, 2010
Copyright this edition © Grub Street 2010

Reprinted 2010

First published in Spanish by Editorial Almuzara,
S.L in 2009 as *La Manzanilla El vino de Sanlúcar*

A CIP catalogue record for this book is available from the
British Library

ISBN 978-1-906502-63-8

Printed and bound in India

This book has been printed on paper from sustainable sources

Contents

Foreword 5

Introduction 7

Where it all Begins 10

The Town of Sanlúcar and the Coto Doñana 25

The Wine and its Name 32

The Production of Manzanilla 44

Where Manzanilla Stands in the Sherry World 60

The Wine People of Sanlúcar 66

    Herederos de Argüeso S.A. 68

    Antonio Barbadillo S.A. 70

    Bodegas Barón S.A. 76

    C.A.Y.D.S.A. 77

    La Cigarrera 79

    Covisan 80

    Delgado Zuleta S.A. 81

    J. Ferris M 83

    Gaspar Florido S.A. 83

    Bodegas Hidalgo – La Gitana 85

    Bodegas Infantes de Orleans-Borbón S.A. 92

Hijos de Rainera Pérez Marín S.A.   94
Bodegas Pedro Romero S.A.   97
Bodegas Sainz de Baranda S.L.   100
Miguel Sánchez Ayala S.A.   100
The Almacenistas of Sanlúcar de Barrameda   101
Other Houses with Manzanilla Interests   105
      Gonzalez Byass y cia.   105
      Emilio Lustau   108
      Bodegas Williams & Humbert S.L.   110
      Other Manzanilla Brands   112
The Gastronomy of Manzanilla   114
Manzanilla and Wine Tourism   136
Manzanilla – Its Future in the World of Wine   141
Glossary   146
Bibliography   151
Hints for the Visitor   154
Index   158

Foreword

Each and every year, more is written about wine, often without adding much that is new and fresh.

Sherry, as it rightly deserves, gets a share of this coverage, but little has been written specifically about the delicious wines known as 'Manzanilla – Sanlúcar de Barrameda', produced on the banks of the Guadalquivir River, and which, to the best of my knowledge, have never been the subject of a book written in English until now.

Manzanilla is affectionately written by an ideal combination of Christopher Fielden, wine merchant, author and pioneer importer of manzanilla and Javier Hidalgo, bodega owner, amateur jockey, and ornithologist. Their shared enthusiasm makes this book a must for anyone wanting to know more about such a fascinating wine.

The stories of manzanilla and the town which is its home, Sanlúcar de Barrameda, are enticingly described in these pages. A glass of the chilled, crisp wine while you read will help you resolve that before long, you too, will go to

Sanlúcar de Barrameda.

Visit the bodegas, taste the wines and then sit on the banks of the Guadalquivir, drinking another glass or two. Enjoy the fresh fish from the bay and watch one of the finest sunsets in Europe.

This slim book holds the key to a special world which I urge you to explore.

Graham Hines, The Sherry Institute.

Introduction

Just a year ago, *La Manzanilla –El vino de Sanlúcar*, written by Javier and myself, was published in Spain. This is not that book, though much of the material is the same. Why have changes been made? Firstly, however traditional the wine trade might appear, it does move on and, for example, there have been changes in the meantime in the ownership of both companies and vineyards. Secondly, some of the material which is relevant to the Spanish reader, is less of interest to a reader in, for example, Britain or the United States. (Here, for example, I am thinking particularly of some of the recipes towards the end of the book, where certain ingredients are not widely available. Does braised coot appeal?) Thirdly, we have tried to make suggestions as to where he or she might stay, eat and, most important of all, sample the subject of this book, for the wine is part of the life of Andalusia and whilst it is at the heart of the picture, it is not the whole picture. Sanlúcar is where the wine is produced, but from there it flows across the Guadalquivir to the Coto Doñana and upstream to Seville... and the rest of the world.

There are both advantages and disadvantages to a book having joint authors. In this case, I consider it a plus that Javier is able to write from the perspective of a lifetime in the sherry trade and the region, whilst I am able to look in from outside. On the other hand, there is the difficulty of expressing personal opinions. It was Javier who wrote the introduction to the Spanish book and in it he said:

> *"In splitting the work between the two of us, Christopher looked after the chapters referring to the history of manzanilla, the place that it has in the world of sherry and the details on the various producing companies. I dealt with the rest. Throughout the text you will find opinions expressed in the first person, which sometimes belong to him and sometimes to me, without the authorship of that chapter being specified."*

The same is still true of this book, though any major differences of opinion may have disappeared as the texts, in Spanish and English, passed between us.

Finally, I would like to thank all who have helped provide the body and soul of this book, be it in opinions, information, hospitality, good company or *copitas* of manzanilla. We have been particularly fortunate to have access to the archives of the late Duchess of Medina Sidonia. She was a formidable personality and will be much missed. The Barbadillo family, who have chronicled manzanilla, both in history and verse, were particularly generous in providing me with source books and each bodega I visited offered me a different perspective on the subject. Finally, this book would not have happened without the support of Jorge Pascual, President of the Consejo Regulador de las Denominaciónes de Origen de Jerez, Manzanilla y Vinagre de Jerez.

Christopher Fielden
February 2010

Where it all Begins

The Guadalquivir, which in Arabic means 'the Great River', is the river of Andalucia. It rises in the Sierra de Cazorla and flows for six hundred kilometres through the cities of Cordoba and Seville to enter the Atlantic Ocean with, at its mouth, on the left bank, as it joins the sea, the town of Sanlúcar de Barrameda and on its right, the vast wilderness of the nature reserve of the Coto Doñana. It is distinctive as being the only navigable river in Spain, with ocean-going boats sailing upstream as far as Seville. This book, though, is not about the river, though it does play a distinctive role, but rather about the town at its mouth and the unique product that has spread its fame around the world, manzanilla.

This position of Sanlúcar has been the root of the town's glorious history, for, here, over the centuries, it has been the first landfall for voyagers from afar and it has been the point of departure for explorers and merchants sailing to the furthest corners of the world. Just beyond the Pillars of Hercules and at the gateway to the Atlantic Ocean it was a strategic site as long as sailing ships were the main means of international transport.

Whilst traditional history has held that it was either the Greeks or the Phoenicians who first introduced the vine to what is now the sherry region, recent archaeological studies have shown that the vine was native to this part of Spain for centuries before their arrival. What is probable is that it was at the time of the Phoenicians that wine-making became general here, for there are remains of amphoras and pressing-troughs which date from that era. It was the classical geographer Strabo, who settled in Rome in about 14AD, who first wrote about these wines and it was he who said the Phoenicians first introduced the vine around 1100BC. Columella, the author of *De Re Rustica*, the great classical treatise on agriculture and viticulture, who also lived during the first century AD, was born on the family estate at Gades, current-day Cádiz.

The rule of the Romans was followed by that of the Visigoths, and, in turn, by that of the Mohammedans from the eighth to the thirteenth century. Whilst the Koran specifically forbade the consumption of alcohol, the production of wine seems to have continued in the region and poets of the time speak of the pleasure to be gained from it. At this time trade was mainly carried out by Jews, of whom there were a considerable number in Andalucia, and who enjoyed a protected status. In 960AD, Al Hakim II decreed that all vineyards should be destroyed, but it was pointed out to him that it would be impossible to prevent the importation of inferior wines from elsewhere, so his decree was never brought into effect.

Whilst we know a reasonable amount about the production of wine in the greater sherry region at this time, no specific mention is made of the wines of Sanlúcar. F.W.C. (F.W.Cozens) in his book *Sherryana*, which appeared at the end of the nineteenth century, quotes *A Diary of the Operations of the Army of Jusuf*, written when he was besieging Jerez in 1288. In this, mention is made of vineyards and gardens to the east of the town, but nothing similar is said when he is fighting around Sanlúcar. From this he deduces that there were none at this time. Whether such a conclusion can be justified, must be unsure.

The Moors were driven out of Sanlúcar in 1264 and thirty-three years later the Lordship of the town was given to Alonso Pérez de Guzmán, 'the Good'. In 1368, his descendants were granted the title of Condes de Niebla and in 1445 that of Duques de Medina Sidonia. From the beginning the town gained important trading rights, including that of holding an annual fair, which attracted merchants from many foreign countries. The Guzmán family recognised the potential of Sanlúcar as a port and privileges were granted to English merchants as early as 1297. Their position in the community was strengthened when the Jews were expelled from Spain in 1492. By 1517, their mercantile role was of sufficient strength that they could ask the then Duke, Alonso de Guzmán, if he would grant them a piece of land in the Ribera quarter of the town, so that they could establish a chapel dedicated to Saint George, where they could bury their dead. This grant of land was confirmed on March 14th of that year and, in 1631, there is mention of a school of the same name.

The importance of the port as the launch pad for explorers must not be under-estimated. It was from here that Columbus set out on his third voyage to the Americas in 1498 and from here that Magellan set sail. It was to here, too, that the last surviving ship of his fleet, under the captaincy of Juan Sebastian Elcano, limped home, thus completing the first circumnavigation of the globe. Its standing as a maritime centre of consequence naturally led to its increasing role in the mercantile world, for boats had to be victualled and supplies put on board to satisfy the needs of the emerging colonies.

In 1530, the English king Henry VIII confirmed the importance of the community of his nationals in Sanlúcar, as being the strongest in all Andalucia, by giving the merchants the right to elect their own Governor, or Consul. Similar rights were also granted over the years to French, Flemish and German merchants, but only the English were permitted to select their own representative; all the other Consuls were appointed by the Duke. This role of Consul carried with it considerable judicial powers.

Whilst Henry's divorce from Catherine of Aragon did not totally sour the trading relations, his renouncing of Catholicism led to pressure on the merchants from the Inquisition and, in 1540, the situation became so bad that the English community, led by their Consul, William Ostrych, laid an official complaint. That these merchants were considered to be of vital importance to the then Duke, is confirmed by the fact that in 1650 Francisco Maldonado de León was appointed by him specifically to look after their interests.

In the following century, one English merchant who had been based in Sanlúcar, became a freebooter. He captured a Spanish galleon, the *San Salvador*, stripped her of her cargo and sent her empty to Seville. With her he sent a covering letter, justifying what he had done by claiming that he was only recouping what he had lost in Sanlúcar.

The archives of the Dukes of Medina Sidonia frequently mention deals with English merchants. In 1561, the then Duke bought a property in the centre of the town from one Thomas Gual. At other times they bought such diverse merchandise as a barrel of salmon, canvas, twelve cheeses and five pieces of artillery. As well as wine, other exports to England included chocolate, presumably imported from Mexico, and orange essence.

As has already been suggested, trading had its ups and downs. In 1579, an increase in the number of English merchants in the town was noted, but with war between the two countries, and Drake's attack on the royal Spanish fleet in Cádiz harbour, commerce between the two countries was forbidden and by 1589 all the merchants had left. However, they were not absent for long and, by 1607, we hear of a merchant John Muídi (perhaps Moody) selling salt cod and, in the following year, another Englishman Thomas Arhal, buying wine. The post of Consul appears to have been reinstated, for at the time it was one Guillermo Davis.

Whilst exports to northern Europe were important for the wine houses of Sanlúcar, the rapidly expanding colonies in the Americas opened up vast new markets for their wines. This led to increased planting of vineyards and to larger stocks of ageing wine being held in the local warehouses, or *bodegas*. So much so that the archives record that, "This leads one to believe that the wine industry is beginning to take off".

For the wine trade an important fact was that, from as early as 1519, the Merchant Venturers of Seville had a right to dictate what should form a proportion of the cargo of any boat sailing for the Americas. This was called the *tercio de frutos* and included not just wine, but also vine-plants. Whilst the wine producers closer to Seville were generally called upon to provide the necessary wines, when Sanlúcar was offered the opportunity to supply them, it was split amongst the growers in proportion to what they produced. However, silting was a regular problem for the Guadalquivir and by the end of the eighteenth century, most of the wine was sent from Sanlúcar to Cádiz for onward shipment.

For just over nine years, at the beginning of the nineteenth century, under the patronage of Manuel de Godoy, twice President of the Council of Ministers, Sanlúcar became the capital of a Province of the same name and the fashionable retreat for the royal family during the summer months. One of the benefits that it gained from this relationship was the re-establishment of the town as a port. The mouth of the river was dredged and new quays constructed at Bonanza, where a magnificent Customs House was built. Sadly, this maritime renaissance was short-lived!

Manuel M. Gonzalez Gordon, in his book *Sherry*, writes, "It is thus essential to place on record that **Jerez alone** is the true cradle of the sherry trade", even though exports were restricted by its comparatively difficult access to the sea. (This problem was not solved until the construction of a railway to the wharves at Trocadero, near Cádiz, in 1853.) Whilst Sr. Gonzalez allows that Puerto de Santa Maria might make a partial claim on its own behalf, he makes no mention at all of Sanlúcar. Why is this?

The fact is that until the beginning of the nineteenth century the wines of Sanlúcar were not generally accepted as being sherries. (In some ways this is hardly surprising for the word sherry is the English corruption of the name of the town where the wines were produced, Jerez.) For example D.M'Bride, writing in 1793, says, "Xerez, or sherry, a good dry white wine, in general use in Britain and much admired. San Lucar, also, is another white wine of the same district, reckoned not so good as sherry but, whether this is owing to the nature of the vine, the soil, or the manner of the making of the wine, is a matter I have not yet been able to ascertain; however there is yearly much more of the San Lucar made than of the sherry; and being cheaper is mixed with the sherry; but, whether mixed or separate, a moderate use of them at table is not unwholesome." Twelve years later, Dr. R. Shannon, in his monumentally titled *A Practical Treatise on Brewing, Distilling, and Rectification... with a Copious Appendix on the culture and preparation of Foreign Wines...*, entitles a chapter 'Sherry and St. Lucar Wines'.

By 1846, when Richard Ford wrote his *Gatherings from Spain*, manzanilla had become accepted as the name for a style of wine from Sanlúcar, though it was still not considered as a sherry. "In Andalucia it was no less easy for the Moor to encourage the use of water as a beverage, than to prohibit that of wine, which, if endued with strength, which sherry is, must destroy health when taken largely and habitually, as is occasionally found in Gibraltar. Hence the natives of Xerez themselves infinitely prefer a light wine called manzanilla, which is made near San Lucar, and is at once much weaker and cheaper than sherry."

Some idea of what wines the merchants of Sanlúcar were offering can be gained from a letter that J.A.Toledo sent, in 1850, from France ordering wines through his friend Manuel de Castro y Alarcón:

"Forgive me for abusing your friendship once again with my problems, but please could you do me the favour of writing to Sanlúcar to order a barrel of Tintilla de Rota of two arrobas. One of the same size of Pedro Ximénez, or of another sweet wine from the region that you consider suitable. In addition to these, I would like a cask of four arrobas, whose name escapes me, but was as good as anything from anywhere in Xerez, which I drank at the house of the Director of Ordales. I want none of these wines to be blended in any way, and they should be shipped from Cádiz in one of the boats sailing for Le Havre. The barrels should be consigned to the Spanish Consul in that town, for forwarding to H.E. The Duke of Sotomayor, the Ambassador of her Royal Highness the Queen in Paris. Please let me know what this will cost, both for the wine and the shipping, in order that I can reimburse you, so that I can have no debts outstanding at the end of this year....

P.S. A friend has told me that the wines of Sanlúcar are very expensive, so I ask you, before buying the wines, to enquire what they will cost and let me know, to see if the prices are acceptable."

(It is interesting to read how perception of the relative cost of wines from Sanlúcar varies over just a four year period.)

A further illustration of the commercial acumen of the

local wine merchants was their ability during the Peninsular War to find customers on both sides of the battle-lines. One company went even so far as to name one range of its products after Napoleon and another after Wellington!

In Britain it seems there was a certain vogue for manzanilla in Victorian times, though not always under that name. As a writer at that time says, "In 1825 the wines from San Lucar came much into vogue. They were pale and received such fanciful names as *rockwater sherry*. But, owing to their want of body and alcoholicity, they gradually had to be assimilated to Xérès wines." Just a few paragraphs earlier, he had described manzanilla as follows: "The wine is rank and common but improves in taste and flavour by keeping. When its fermentation is perfect, it is of light body, light colour, and has great lasting qualities; but withal it is so peculiar, that a person unaccustomed to it would believe it to be a medicinal tincture rather than a wine, and require some length of time to habituate himself to its enjoyment." It seems surprising, in the circumstances, that such an unattractive wine should have become fashionable.

Apropos of the medicinal taste, there is the story of an, unspecified, Earl of Derby being prescribed manzanilla for his gout. He purchased a bottle from his wine merchant, but, within the space of days returned it almost full, with an accompanying message to the effect that of the two he preferred gout.

One of the strongest promoters of manzanilla was the French author Prosper Merimée – the wine even gets a mention in his best-known work *Carmen*. In 1864, writing to his friend Panizzi about life in Madrid, he says that the quality of the sherry on the market is "detestable. The only wine that is drinkable is manzanilla, but the only people who drink it are the Andalucians, the tarts and me."

It would seem therefore that the end of the eighteenth century and the first half of the nineteenth were a crucial time for Sanlúcar and its wines. Flor appeared for the first time and this in turn led to the creation of the solera system and these happened in Sanlúcar, before the rest of the region. These developments, and the effects of the sea breezes from the Atlantic, gave the individual character to the local wine, manzanilla. It was about this time, also, that the shipment for export of all wines from the region came to be concentrated on Cádiz and the wines of Sanlúcar were absorbed into the sherry family.

There seem to have been two waves in the creation of the companies that we see on the market today. In the eighteenth century there was a process of evolution from winemaker to wine merchant. At the same time there was a drive to populate Andalucia, by encouraging immigrants from the north of Spain. During this century we see the foundation of Delgado Zuleta (1744), La Cigarrera (1758) and Hidalgo (1792). The increasing vogue for the wine in the following century saw the arrival of Barbadillo (1821), Herederos de Argüeso (1822), Bodegas Barón (1871) and Florido Hermanos (1880).

Phylloxera arrived in the vineyards of Sanlúcar in 1894 and, as in most of the wine regions of Europe at that time, it had a disastrous effect. Calculations based on historical records show that the average annual production of wine in the town fell from 24,000 butts to no more than 500. As a result of this, many of the more marginal companies went out of business or were absorbed by their stronger competitors.

What has been described by the leading local writer on the subject, Ana María Gómez, as the First Golden Age for manzanilla came to an end in approximately 1920. For her, the Second Golden Age began in the early 80's. From 1950 until 1980, however, sales of manzanilla declined and it suffered from a serious image problem. In the meantime there were sherry successes in two different directions. On the domestic market and, to a much smaller extent on foreign markets, fino was king, led by Tio Pepe from the Gonzalez Byass stable, but followed by such wines as La Ina from Domecq and Garvey's San Patricio. In Anglo-Saxon markets and particularly in Britain, Bristol Cream came from nowhere to capture the housewife's imagination. This, in turn led to the creation of a totally new style of sherry by the marketing department of International Distillers and Vintners, pale cream. This new child, Croft's Original, was an overnight success. These two cream sherries now account for more than half the sherry sales on the British market, just over a million cases a year. (To put things in perspective, the total annual sherry sales in Spain are approximately 1.5 million cases a year.)

The success of Harvey's Bristol Cream also led to more baleful consequences for the sherry trade and particularly so in Sanlúcar. When William Perry founded the company that was to become Harvey's of Bristol in 1796, he specialised in wines from the Iberian Peninsula and his company soon became known for the quality of its sherries. In due course their leading brand became Bristol Cream, which has changed in style somewhat over the years. In their price-list of 1958, which I have in front of me, it is described as "choicest old full pale". Coincidentally, it was in that same year that they first signed a contract for the sourcing of some of their wine requirements, to be shipped in bulk for bottling in Bristol, with Zoilo Ruiz-Mateos, an *almacenista* in Jerez.

Six years later, he was granted a hundred-year contract for the exclusive supply of all their sherries. This was a licence to print money and, a few years later, when Harvey's was taken over by the Showering family, the contract was cancelled and a substantial sum was paid in compensation to Sr. Ruiz-Mateos. At the time, Spain was undergoing a period of severe financial depression and, on the back of the money that he had at his disposal, an empire was created in the worlds of banking, hotels and wine. In this last field, he bought up many over-extended companies in Rioja and the sherry region. Trade in Sanlúcar was particularly depressed and he quickly purchased a number of bodegas including Hijos de A. Pérez Megia and Otaolaurruchi.

To add to all this, the story became prevalent that manzanilla was too delicate a wine to be exported. Whilst it was a wine to be enjoyed in Spain, and more especially in Andalucia, it was little more than a local novelty. This was an easy rumour to create and dissipate, as manzanilla has tended to lay stress on its individual merit of lightness and the fact that it should be consumed as soon as possible after bottling. He who sells manzanilla treads a delicate path! This image frightened a number of potential consumers. I can remember visiting a bar, one of a major chain that, at the time, based its reputation on selling a broad range of sherries directly from the cask. I ordered a 'dock glass' of manzanilla and, after a search that must have lasted a good fifteen minutes, a bottle was produced that, I am convinced, had not seen a customer in the previous twelve months. It is stating the obvious to say that this wine did nothing for the reputation of manzanilla!

It was perhaps just as well for the vineyard owners and

sherry producers of Sanlúcar that their brothers in Jerez were not suffering to the same extent, as potential manzanillas became the base wine for many of the leading finos. Notwithstanding the difficulties the producers were going through, they stood out for the individuality of their product and it was granted its own *Denominación de Origen* (D.O.) in 1964.

What were the factors that led to the Second Golden Age? Paradoxically, one was the nature of the wine; what had, for the past thirty years or so, appeared to be its major weakness, now became its major attraction. The consumer was tiring of heavy, fortified sweet wines and began to look for something less alcoholic and more refreshing. The producers in Sanlúcar were not slow in perceiving which way the wind was blowing and many of the leading brands which for generations had been manzanillas pasadas, overnight became manzanillas finas. Brands like La Guita were revitalised by marketing teams that had learnt their art in the Rumasa Group of Sr.Ruiz-Mateos.

In export markets such as Britain and Germany, considerable impetus to the wines was given when the minimum alcoholic strength for the export of finos and amontillados was reduced to 15%. This put them into lower bands of taxation and effectively either reduced their price to the consumer or released money for promotion. In Britain, this coincided with a time when the pound was strong against the euro, leading to a period of price stability. This concept of the changing image of sherry in general and manzanilla in particular, is not restricted to the poster hoardings. Gonzalez Byass, for its fino brand Tio Pepe, was the first to try to re-present the product as a table wine rather than as a sherry. The bottle style changed dramatically and the label featured the grape variety, the palomino, for the first time. The image of Tio Pepe as a new-style, new-world, varietal wine was born. Two leading manzanilla brands, Solear of Barbadillo and La Gitana of Hidalgo soon also sought to achieve a similar image by introducing individual bottle styles for their wines.

The recent fashion for consumption of the wine that includes Sanlúcar in its title appears to have done little to benefit this bustling town of just over sixty thousand inhabitants. Historically it has relied on two sources of employment, fishing and agriculture, with those employed in the former living along the river bank in the Bajo de Guía quarter and those in the latter, in the upper town. It is the world of agriculture that has suffered most, with hundreds of hectares of sherry vineyards grubbed up, in a bid to match supply to demand. Where there were once vineyards, there are now plastic polytunnels where flowers and early vegetables are grown.

Tourists are attracted to the sandy Atlantic beaches and to the three big events in the Sanluqueño calendar: the *Feria de manzanilla*, which takes place each May; *El Rocio*, an annual two-week long pilgrimage at Pentecost to a shrine in the Doñana National Park, when thousands of pilgrims on horseback and in horse-drawn wagons, well laden with the local produce, queue up to catch the ferry across the Guadalquivir; and the horse-races that take place at the end of August and beginning of September. They have the distinction of being the country's oldest regulated races, but also of being one of only two places in Europe where the races, tides permitting, take place on the beach. For some reason, however, the tourists are mainly Spanish. The rest of Europe seems more attracted to the Costa de Sol to the east or the Algarve, to the west.

Whilst there are some bodegas that are immediately apparent to the passing motorist, most of them are hidden away down the narrow cobbled streets that comprise the town. Here oeno-tourism has been slow to become the commercial factor that it is in Jerez. Manzanilla is for drinking in the multitude of tapas bars that stud the town, but more particularly in those that line the quays at Bajo de Guía.

The Town of
Sanlúcar and the
Coto Doñana

"For us, the Coto Doñana has always seemed to be a fragment of the wild solitude of Africa, carved out and specially prepared for our enjoyment in this remote corner of Spain. For us, hunters, naturalists and lovers of wild deserts, Doñana represents no less than paradise on earth..." This was how Abel Chapman, a British sportsman and ornithologist, described early in the last century, what may well be today the most important nature reserve in Europe. Chapman was born in Sunderland in 1851 and it was the wine trade that brought him to Jerez, where he made friends with Walter John Buck. Both loved to shoot and to explore wild, little-visited corners of Spain. At the turn of the century they wrote two books (*Wild Spain*, 1893 and *Unexplored Spain*, 1910) which are considered to be true jewels and valuable source-books about the natural history of that time.

Doñana, separated from Sanlúcar by no more than the river, is a wide area with on one side the Atlantic Ocean as its boundary and, on the other, the river Guadalquivir. These two factors have created a complex eco-system dominated by marshes and sand-dunes. Today it is protected by its dual status as a National Park and a Biosphere Reserve.

In the remote times of the Pliocene era, this was one vast marine gulf, which became sealed off into a coastal lagoon into which the river deposited its sediment, before forming a broad estuary. Thus the geological history of Doñana was born out of these two agents, the river and the sea.

We have seen how manzanilla depends on its individual microclimate, which comes from its geographical situation. It is precisely this coming together of the sea, river and marshes that is responsible for this microclimate, without which this individual wine would not have its distinct character.

Although Doñana belongs administratively to the province of Huelva, throughout its history access to it has been across the river from Sanlúcar. For many centuries, Doñana was a royal hunting reserve, tied to the Dukes of Medina Sidonia, the Lords of Sanlúcar. Nowadays it is a National Park, controlled by the government. The gamekeepers responsible for protecting the park, have always, for reasons of closeness, been natives of Sanlúcar.

In the town of Sanlúcar, Doñana is always known as "the other side", that is to say the other side of the river. Its beach, thirty kilometres of virgin sand, was considered as a possible landing point for D-day, in the Second World War.

"The other side" plays an important role in the whole panorama that is the beach at Sanlúcar. The combination of the mouth of the river in the foreground and the sand-dunes crowned by Mediterranean pine-trees in the background, creates a remarkable panoply of colours. This is particularly so at sunset, leaving an unforgettable imprint on the minds of all visitors to the town. An extra feature at the end of each month of August, is the famous horse-races along the beach. These are the oldest in Spain, having first been run in 1845. Since then they have been governed by rules borrowed from the Jockey Club of Great Britain. This picture of the horses galloping along the beach, with the river and its boats and the Doñana as a backdrop, with occasionally, as an added feature, a flock of flamingos or other water-birds passing by, has led to this sporting event being awarded the official title of "Tourist attraction of International Interest".

The race meetings are not just a sporting event, they are also a major social occasion, for every family, association and company in the town holds a reception in their individual multi-coloured canvas pavilions at which their friends, guests and customers are all welcome. Each pavilion maintains the tradition of providing its personal style of sandwich or tapa, all washed down with a *caña* of manzanilla. This is further evidence of the close bonds that link manzanilla and the sea to which it owes so much. Here during race-nights hundreds of bottles of manzanilla are drunk during the festivities, which follow the races themselves, and which continue until the dawn. It is no more than logical that it is here that manzanilla shows itself at its best, for it is here that it is conceived and comes to life.

At the western end of the beach of Sanlúcar, just opposite

the temporary grandstand by the winning post, there appears what seems to be a rocky track into the middle of the river, which opens out into a broader heap of rocks; the haunt of those seeking crabs and of rod-fishermen. These are the remains of a fort, the Castillo del Espiritu Santo, which acted as a lookout point for ships. Its destruction during the nineteenth century, brings back memories of unhappy alliances for the townsfolk of Sanlúcar. This was during the Peninsular War when the only supplies breaking the blockade that Napoleon had put around Britain, came either from the Guadalquivir or certain Portuguese ports. However, when the Napoleonic forces drove into the south of Spain, the British feared that the French might occupy the fort and thus control the shipping from the river. A fleet was therefore dispatched to demolish the fort. The local inhabitants were disappointed that their allies, to whom they had sent supplies, should be the ones responsible for this destruction. The hope still lingers on, however, that those who destroyed the fort will some day come to repair it... (As has already been mentioned, however, the Sanluquenos were wise enough not to put all their eggs in one basket. They were happy to supply the French, as well as the British, with sherry.)

On the left bank of the river, the system of dunes and marshes is similar to that of the Doñana, but here there have been many changes. Sanlúcar has created here a pine wood known as La Algaida on top of the dunes and you can find similar flora and fauna to that on the other side of the river. The marshes in Sanlúcar have been largely drained and salt-pans have been created for the production of common sea-salt, by evaporation. The salt-pans are the oldest in the Bay of Cádiz. It was Carlos III, in the eighteenth century, who ordered the construction of those of Santa Teresa.

At that time salt was a valuable commodity and not easy to find. Quays were constructed, so that the salt could be shipped up-river to Seville, mainly to be used for the preservation of olives, or downstream to the sea, for onward shipment to other markets. For the production of salt, vast quantities of sea water are needed and this is fed into the salt-pans through sluices at high-tide. It is then left to evaporate in the sun, until the salt crystallises.

The process requires vast expanses of shallow water, which make an ideal habitat for a large number of birds. In this way the salt-pans act as host to a rich variety of waterfowl and waders, particularly during the summer, when the pans dry out.

It can be said that this local industry also contributes something to the saltiness that is generally perceived in the flavour of manzanilla. Whether this be true or not, salt is certainly one of the basic elements that goes to make up Sanlúcar.

On both sides of the river, between the dunes there are sandy depressions, known locally as *corrales* or *navazos* and, on the Sanlúcar side this is where the vine nurseries have traditionally been planted. Being sheltered from the wind, by being below the level of the dunes, and by having light, friable soil, these create an ideal site for the growth of the young vines.

The importance of the Doñana marsh complex cannot be under-estimated as far as nature is concerned. On the one hand this enclave is where the two continents come together, and its individual nature makes it home to a rich fauna, with such icon species as the lynx and the imperial eagle. In addition to this, it is situated right on the route of migratory birds between Europe and Africa, precisely at that point which is a bottle-neck for winged traffic. Its position, so close to the Straits of Gibraltar, makes it a logical place of rest and recuperation for the birds during their long flight.

Additionally, the marshes and the brushwood and pine forests of Doñana, provide the ideal winter home for many birds from central and northern Europe, who would not be able to survive in their homelands. Thus, during the winter months it is the home of thousands of ducks, geese, cranes and other birds.

This rich and varied fauna, particularly in birds, has attracted many visitors over the centuries. These have been mainly foreigners and often British. Many of these have written about what they have found and this has led to even further visitors: in early days what can almost be described as explorers and more recently naturalists and sportsmen. Others were jointly drawn by the wines of the region and it is interesting to note that the first written mentions of Doñana and its attractions date back to the arrival of British wine traders in the 18th and 19th centuries.

Ornithology and field-sports, particularly shooting, brought these visitors to Doñana and some of them purchased shooting rights in the region. Apart from the works of Abel Chapman, which have already been mentioned, perhaps the most important, with regard to spreading knowledge to the wider scientific world of this former royal hunting reserve, was *Portrait of a Wilderness, The Story of the Coto Doñana Expeditions*, by Guy Mountford, which was published in 1958. Over time, much has changed for Doñana; it has gone from the exclusive preserve of the royal family to become a National Park and a centre for scientific exploration.

Sanlúcar and Doñana are not just linked by the Guadalquivir that runs between them and the microclimate that they share. They are bound by the interests of the visitors, the ornithologists, the sportsmen and the winelovers, many of whom have shared their feelings in books. Manzanilla, the river, Sanlúcar and the Coto Doñana are not separate entities. They are inextricably linked and they all thrive on each other. They all benefit from this symbiosis.

Whilst Sanlúcar is situated at the southern fringe of Doñana, at the northern extremity can be found El Rocío, a hamlet that has grown up around a shrine, that of Nuestra Señora del Rocío, which is the site of one of the oldest religious traditions of Andalucia. Each year, around Pentecost, a caravan of riders and carts drawn by mules and oxen, sets out from Sanlúcar and crosses the river on a pilgrimage across Doñana, reaching its climax with the annual visit to the Virgin at her shrine. The journey, of forty-five kilometres, through the dunes and pine forests is accomplished in three days. The days are passed in riding and, at evening, camp is pitched and it becomes a time for singing, dancing and drinking manzanilla. Dress is the elegant typical clothing of Andalucia and the men ride with their women sitting sideways on the rump of the horse. This makes for one of the most colourful and unexpected pictures of Doñana.

Hundreds of these caravans, from all parts of Andalucia and from further afield in Spain, converge on El Rocío and, for three days, homage is paid to the White Dove, the Queen of the Marshes, Nuestra Senora del Rocío. Then all return by the same tracks through the wilderness. It is the various Brotherhoods of the south of Spain, who, each year, cross the Doñana on this pilgrimage. They follow a route with no roads, no towns and no houses, apart from the few hunters' lodges. Most important of all, the sole official drink on this pilgrimage is manzanilla.

The Wine
and its Name

The current renown of the town of Sanlúcar undoubtedly
comes through its role as the nursery of the wine that is
known as manzanilla, or, to give it its full and proper title,
Manzanilla-Sanlúcar de Barrameda, a full *denominación de
origen* under the Spanish law. Why I say 'nursery' and not
'birthplace' will soon be made clear.

As Manuel Barbadillo Rodríguez has written, "Sanlúcar
and manzanilla are names that are intertwined, that join
and meld together in a lifelong, harmonious marriage."
There is one distinction about this wine, as opposed to, as
far as I know, every other geographical wine name in the
world: it is not where the grapes come from that is important, but, rather, where the resultant wine is aged. Not only

this, but only certain styles of wine have right to the name. (Somewhat similar is the liqueur Cassis de Dijon. For that the fruit can come from anywhere, often eastern Europe, but the fruit has to be turned into the end product in that Burgundian town.)

The relationship between manzanilla and sherry is a complex and seemingly perverse one and will be explained in more detail later, but to put it as simply as possible, "manzanilla is a dry wine produced from grapes grown within the delimited area of production for sherry, but aged in a bodega within the town of Sanlúcar." The maritime climate, with cooling onshore Atlantic breezes, means the wine ages differently from other sherries and takes on certain distinctive characteristics. John Arlott, the wine-writer and sports commentator, summed these up in an article in *The Guardian* in July 1971. "Manzanilla is another matter. Although by Spanish law it is a sherry, it has a completely different, and quite unique, aroma and dry flavour, said to derive from the salty sea winds that blow across the vineyards near Sanlúcar de Barrameda. Manzanilla has its own devotees, especially among Spaniards, who drink it exclusively, in preference to sherry." One of those devotees was John himself, who, in retirement on the island of Alderney, always had a bottle within reach. However much he might have appreciated the wine, what he wrote was not exactly the truth; it is not the effect of the sea breezes on the vineyards that is important, but rather the effect that they have on the wine during the long years that it is ageing, that gives it its distinctive characteristics.

Every wine that calls itself manzanilla can, if it so desires, call itself sherry, but there are comparatively few sherries that can call themselves manzanilla. Over the centuries, the trade in sherry has been dominated by the big, now often multi-national, companies based in Jerez de la Frontera, but, as forecast by John Arlott, tastes have changed and it is the wines of Sanlúcar that have come into vogue. This fashion started on the Spanish domestic market and is now slowly spreading around the world.

The next chapter will deal in more detail about the production of sherry and more especially manzanilla, but suffice it to say that within the world of sherries there are two basic 'sexes', the finos and the olorosos. Historically, the factors that led to the conception of the two styles lay with nature; now science plays a larger part and, as with the sex of unborn children, the style can now be pre-determined. There is no doubt that this has been a great help in enabling the producers to satisfy the rapid increase in demand for manzanilla from the world markets, for it can only be born as a fino. Thus, while the current taste is predominantly for wines that are young, light and fresh, *manzanillas finas*, it is also possible to have fuller-bodied *manzanillas pasadas* or even *manzanillas amantilladas*, though, by that stage, there is little difference between a true *amantillado* aged in Sanlúcar and one aged in Jerez.

How does an individual sherry produced in Sanlúcar come ever to be called manzanilla? That is a question that has filled many pages in wine books for the past century or more and I wish I could come up with a definitive answer. The Spanish dictionary that I have used for the past fifty years or so credits the word *manzanilla* with a broad variety of meanings, beginning with 'a certain white wine from Andalucia'. Next comes 'camomile' – and there is always the danger in Spain of when you order a manzanilla, you're receiving a *copita* of sherry, when you wanted a herb-tea, or vice-versa. It also can be 'a variety of olive', 'an architectural decoration in the form of a pineapple', or even 'the lower part of a beard'. Despite this rich vein of alternative sources, there are three distinct schools of thought as to how this wine came to be named.

Here are the differing arguments as put forward by three different writers at three different times:

> ***Manzanilla****: The best sherry of the San Lucar vineyards, west of Jerez de la Frontera. It is, or should be, pale of colour, dry of finish and with a peculiar and attractive crab-apple flavour. Hence the name of manzanilla, small apples.*
>
> *A Dictionary of Wine*, André Simon, 1935.

> ***Manzanilla*** *or **Mançanilla***: *A superior brand of new sherry, remarkably dry, and a delicate tonic, produced between San Lucar de Barrameda and Jerez de la Frontera, in Spain, Its name is the Spanish word for camomile, the flavour of which it possesses. Colour: light straw. This wine is the purest made; and an admixture would spoil it.*
>
> *Law's Grocer's Manual*, circa 1901.

> ***Manzanilla****: The driest and, when young, palest of sherries is grown and matured in the area of Sanlúcar de Barrameda, a coastal town twelve miles from Jerez, whence Columbus once set sail for America and Magellan for the Pacific. Manzanilla is bone dry, with a hint of bitterness and a tang attributed to the sea air: if taken inland to mature in Jerez it loses this tang, and similarly, fino wine fer-*

mented in Jerez acquires the tang if matured in Sanlúcar. Manzanilla is the Spanish word for the camomile, but the wine is named after a village in the district, not after the flower; it bears no semblance to the camomile infusion once favoured by invalids. Manzanilla is an elegant wine, but far too dry to be popular.

A Word Book of Wine, Walter James, 1959.

The first suggestion, and the one that one comes across least often is, perhaps, the easiest to dismiss; that manzanilla is a diminutive form of the word *manzana*, an apple. The reasoning is that the wine has an appley taste, or, perhaps even one of a crab-apple. Whilst *–illa* is an occasional diminutive suffix in Spanish, a small apple would more probably be *manzanita*. The Spanish for crab-apple, my dictionary tells me, is *manzana silvestre*.

As for the camomile theory, there is strong support in one of the earliest written mentions of manzanilla as a wine, in the works of a Spanish writer. Esteban Boutelou, and his better-known brother Claudio, were Spain's leading horticulturalists at the beginning of the nineteenth century. Educated in England, they collaborated on a number of books and, in the autumn of 1803, Esteban was appointed Director of the Botanical Gardens at Sanlúcar, by Manuel de Godoy, the Chief Minister in Spain, who has been described variously as the lover or favourite of Queen Maria Luisa. Esteban came to love Sanlúcar and lived there until his death in 1814. His seminal work, *Memoria sobre el cultivo de la vid en Sanlúcar de Barrameda y Xerez de la Frontera* was published in Madrid in 1807.

On page 123, he talks of the Listán grape, then widely

grown for the production of sherry, giving wines that are outstanding for their smell of *manzanilla*, presumably camomile. However, later in the book, on a number of occasions he talks of '*los vinos de manzanilla*'. It is apparent from what he says that he is talking about a style of wine, as he compares their fermentation and development in cask to other wines. On page 146, he writes, "The manzanilla wines must be very clear, white, with no hint of colour, transparent, crystalline, highly flavoured, smooth and soft on the palate: they should be low in strength, but warm the stomach." It is sad that he does not describe the flavour more fully.

Another early writer, Richard Ford, in his *Gatherings in Spain* (1846), also favours the camomile theory. He wrote: "The origin of the name has been much discussed; those who prefer the sound of it to its meaning, tie it to *manzana*, and if it were a cider, that would be acceptable; others link it to the distant town of Mansanilla (sic) on the other side of the river, where it is neither made nor drunk. The true etymology comes from its surprising resemblance to the bitter camomile flower (*manzanilla*) that our doctors use to make a medicinal tea and which those from Spain use to make a stimulant."

The third suggested origin of the name manzanilla is that it comes from the small town of that name, which lies on the main road, the N472, to the west of Seville, coincidentally, just twenty kilometres beyond the town of Sanlúcar la Mayor. This Manzanilla lies within the wine D.O. region of Condado de Huelva, which traditionally has produced *vinos generosos* similar in style to sherries. Indeed, the *Guía Peñin* describes the Condado Pálido as being "quite similar too the other finos of Andalucia (sherries and montillas). It is made from the palomino grape (the main grape in Huelva is the zalema), the same as used in Jerez, though it gives wine of a lesser quality." Indeed, there is a bodega still operating in the town provocatively called *Vinícola Manzanillera*! The archives of the Duchess of Medina Sidonia record that, centuries ago wines were transported on mules from manzanilla to Sanlúcar de Barrameda for onward shipment.

Tommy Layton tells in *Wines and Castles of Spain*, how he had been told by Manuel Barbadillo of the eponymous sherry house, that "the word came from the fact that *manzanilla* is Spanish for camomile and the wine possesses the apple-like scent of this creeping white herb". (This answer appears neatly to embrace two different reasons for the origin of the name.) Despite this, Mr. Layton wrote to the mayor of Manzanilla to seek his opinion on the matter. Perhaps not surprisingly, he replied that his town produced quality wine that historically had been shipped to sherry producers and particularly to those of Sanlúcar de Barrameda. They, in a moment of surprising honesty, had taken the decision to call the wine what it really was – manzanilla.

Sr. Barbadillo has written elsewhere, in more detail, about this whole question and it is interesting to see how he weighs the matter up and how he casts his final vote. "It is logical that wine names should refer to their place of birth and given the fact that the town called Manzanilla, in the Province of Huelva, was situated within the domains of the Duke of Medina Sidonia and then, between 1803 and 1813, in the Province of Sanlúcar, it is possible, and this is what some believe, that the wine now produced in Sanlúcar, manzanilla, owes its name to this fact. However this is unlikely, given the fact that the sixth Duke specifically forbade the importation of *rociado* wines from Huelva."

(The meaning of the word *rociado* is not totally clear; it generally means adding wines to a cask during the solera process. Why the Duke should forbid the importation is also unclear. Logic would seem to suggest that they might be used for mixing with the local wine.)

He continues, "When Sanlúcar was the capital of the province of the same name, Godoy brought the leading botanists and experts of Spain to improve the quality of the vineyards and the production of the wines, one of which, a white wine, smelt distinctly of the herb *manzanilla*. Wines were produced in the town of Manzanilla, in the County of Huelva but they were never given the name of the town."

As a matter of interest, it must be mentioned that wines from the neighbourhood of Manzanilla and the County of Niebla were exported to England as early as the fifteenth century, and during the sixteenth century, Seville was their most important market. A royal decree of 1778 permitted the free movement of wines from other regions to be shipped through Sanlúcar. This decree superceded those of the Dukes of Medina Sidonia, which, as Sr. Barbadillo said, specifically prohibited the importation of such wines into the town. Certainly, the Dukes had regularly bought wines from Lucena, a town within the Huelva area of production and there are documents that show that in 1600 some from there were specifically produced for the then Duchess. The town archives of Manzanilla show that wines from the town were regularly sent to Sanlúcar in the period 1780-1810.

During the eighteenth century, the town of Moguer, at the mouth of the Tinto River, became the principal port for the shipment of Huelva wines; the only permitted alternative being Seville. However the principal role of these ports was to make shipments to the other ports of Spain; all shipments to other countries had to pass through Cádiz.

Nevertheless, for the producers of Manzanilla and neighbouring towns such as Villalba, the easiest route for the transportation of the wines was to avoid Moguer and Seville. They sent the barrels of their wine by cart through Hinojos and Aznalcázar to the creek of las Nueve Suertes. There they were loaded on barges and shipped downstream to where the creek joined the Guadalquivir, near Sanlúcar salt-pans. It is logical they would pass through Sanlúcar and probably would be sold by the merchants who were based there and who had established good contacts with the outside market.

All this is not circumstantial evidence that the wine took the name of the town, but it lends a great deal of strength to this theory. Moreover it appears most unlikely that any native of Sanlúcar would openly accept that the wine that has made the reputation of his town ever came from elsewhere!

Recent research by Alberto Ramos Santana would seem to cast further doubt on Sr. Barbadillo's conclusions. He has discovered mentions of the wines in the works of the Cádiz writer Juan Ignacio González del Castillo, dating back to the end of the eighteenth century, before Godoy arrived in Sanlúcar and the town of Manzanilla was within the Province of Sanlúcar de Barrameda.

It is interesting that this should appear in the works of a Cádiz writer, for the term manzanilla seems to have been current in that town before it is recorded in Sanlúcar archives. There, the first mention is of four butts being shipped to Naples in 1825. Sr. Barbadillo has studied the sales ledgers of a number of Sanlúcar merchants. The first mention of manzanilla in the books of the company Alonso Ximénez Barbudo, which was then known as Dámaso Manuel García de Velasco, is as late as 1864. From then on, it is mentioned every year. However in the records of the house of José Gutiérrez de Aguera, it is mentioned as early as 1839, but only on five occasions in the following decade. In the 1855 inventory of Francisco Gil de Ledesma Sotomayor, now Delgado Zuleta, there are no less than eight different qualities of manzanilla in stock, valued at from 34 to 45 *reales* per *arroba*.

Whatever the origins of the name, there is no doubt that the wines of Sanlúcar led a separate existence from those of Jerez de la Frontera and generally were not considered as sherries, but rather as lighter wines. One of the fathers of the wine industry in Australia, and later New Zealand, James Busby, spent three months in the autumn and winter of 1831 visiting vineyards in Spain and Portugal. His trip began in Cádiz and his diary entry for September 28th notes, "We stopped at a *venta*, or public-house, to obtain a glass of the wine called Manzinilla (sic), the *vin de pays* of the district, which Dr. Wilson assures me is preferred to all other wines by people of all ranks in the country; it is not known in the cellars of the English merchants, but is a light pleasant beverage, having at the same time a mellowness and flavour, which I have no doubt, would after a little habit, procure for it the preference of even those who would find it insipid at the first trial." It is not clear whether Busby, when he speaks of the English merchants, means those in Jerez and Sanlúcar, or those in London and elsewhere, but this suggests even one hundred and seventy years ago, manzanilla was for drinking by the locals whilst sherries were exported.

What then is the present image of manzanilla and is that image distinct from that of sherry? These are two separate questions. Manzanilla would like to be considered as a wine which is light, refreshing and, above all popular and fashionable; an image that appeals to young, new wine-drinkers, those with money to spend. It feels that to achieve such an image it needs to cut itself off from sherry, whose traditional profile has been diametrically opposed to this.

In Spain, this metamorphosis has largely been achieved, but Spain was largely a country of fino drinkers and the rapid increase in sales of manzanilla has largely been at the expense of finos. (This is why Gonzalez Byass have revamped the packaging of Tio Pepe and withdrawn their manzanilla brand El Rocío.) In export markets, however, manzanilla has been seen as just another (minor) type of sherry, with all that implies. On the British market, for example, sherry sales are dominated by two sweet brands, with the majority of sales taking place in the run-up to Christmas. Whilst three manzanilla companies, Argüeso, Barbadillo and Hidalgo, with the support of the regional government of Andalucia, joined together to raise the awareness in the mind of the consumer of the distinct merits of their style of wine, the budget was limited and it is still considered to be a niche sherry. Moreover, in Britain, manzanilla is best appreciated well-chilled, in summer – a time when there is a host of alternative drinks on offer and a type of sherry is an unlikely first choice. In addition, with the move to a healthier lifestyle, a wine of 15° is considered by most to be too heavy. It is an impossible task to convert the traditional sherry drinker in Britain from Bristol Cream to Solear or San León. You might change the Tio Pepe drinker, but for manzanilla really to succeed, it must find new drinkers. It is for this reason that it is seeking if not a divorce, but at least a separation from sherry.

This parting of the ways cannot be an easy one. The history of manzanilla is intimately interwoven with that of sherry. Every producer of manzanilla also offers a broad range of other sherries, perhaps more in export markets than in Spain itself. He may rely on these, and related products, such as brandy and vinegar, for a considerable proportion of his profits. (Indeed, the top-selling dry white table-wine in Spain is Castillo de San Diego, produced by Barbadillo.) Because of demand, every sherry producer, be he in Jerez de la Frontera or Puerto de Santa María, now finds that his Spanish customers are clamouring for manzanilla. These demands must be satisfied, either by establishing a bodega in Sanlúcar, or by buying wine there in bulk. To achieve success in the wine-consuming countries around the world, vast sums of money must be spent – and the multinationals have their outposts in Jerez rather than in Sanlúcar, Additionally, the sherry producers as a group are happy to spend their money on the generic product, rather than on a wine which comes only from one part of the region. It is easier to suggest new ways of drinking cream sherry, which is comparatively cheap to produce, perhaps, for example as an ingredient of mixed drinks, than it is to extol the virtues of manzanilla. (Though it has been suggested that manzanilla makes an ideal replacement for vodka in a Bloody Mary!)

The most likely outcome for this relationship is cohabitation, with neither of the partners being totally happy. Things move very slowly in the south of Spain and the rapid success of manzanilla in the domestic market took many traditional producers by surprise. Inevitably there have been internal jealousies and squabbles, particularly when decisions have to be made as to how promotional money should be spent. Sherry and manzanilla may make uneasy bedfellows, but they must resign themselves to sharing the same pillow.

The Production of Manzanilla

Like every other wine, manzanilla is born in the vineyards, but unlike most other controlled appellation wines, it does not have its own limited area of production, or, rather it can have the whole sherry area as its source. Whilst about 10% of the total area of sherry production lies within the boundaries of the town of Sanlúcar de Barrameda, these have no special standing as far as manzanilla is concerned. In his book which has already been mentioned, Manuel González Gordon lists twenty-seven distinct vineyards within these boundaries, with two particular sites, or *pagos*, Miraflores and Torrebreva, being singled out as the best sources for base-grapes for manzanilla.

On the other hand, Isidro García del Barrio Ambrosy, in

an article entitled *The Many Names of the Campos of Sanlúcar*, lists ninety-nine named vineyards. Interestingly Torrebreva is not included but Miraflores Alta and Miraflores Baja are listed separately. Other names include La Callejuela, Rematacaudales, Charruado, Cabeza Grande, Atalaya, Amarguillo and La Cañada. These all benefit from the onshore breezes which have a cooling influence during the heat of the summer.

The reason why there is an apparent conflict between what has been written by these two authors is that whilst Torrebreva may be an ideal source pago for base wine for manzanilla, it does not lie within the boundaries of the municipality of Sanlúcar de Barrameda, but rather in Rota. As it is the property of the Monpensier family, whose bodega is in Sanlúcar, much of the resultant product is manzanilla.

An interesting early visitor to Sanlúcar was Henry Vizetelly, the author and publisher, who was later to be imprisoned for publishing a translation of Emile Zola's 'obscene' novel *La Terre*. He was for a time a correspondent for *The Illustrated London News* and could claim to be the grandfather of illustrated wine books. In 1876 he visited the sherry region and paid a visit to the Torrebreva vineyard at vintage time. He gives a detailed description of the property, which though it belonged to the Duc de Monpensier at the time, was leased by a certain Mr. Davies, an English wine merchant from Jerez.

"Dotting the vineyards are groups of white outbuildings, and starting up in various directions are little huts of esparto, perched upon four poles, and to which access is obtained by aid of a short ladder. These are so many look-out places for the half-dozen

guards, who, armed with old-fashioned Moorish firelocks, are employed to watch the vineyards from the commencement of July until the vintage is over, and are after the same fashion as corresponding structures encountered throughout the Médoc."

"Upwards of 200 men were occupied with the vintage at Torre Breva. Advocates of women's rights will regret to hear that the labours of the softer sex are altogether dispensed with in the vineyards of the South of Spain."

The concept of selling wines under single vineyard names is only rarely used for sherries, though, on higher quality wines, the name of the pago is occasionally mentioned. As far as manzanillas are concerned the one that is regularly seen is the Pastrana Manzanilla Pasada of Hidalgo and Gaspar Florido also sell some wines under the vineyard name of Viña Armijo. Both Pastrana and Viña Armijo form part of the pago of Miraflores.

The neatness of the Sanlúcar vineyards is striking. Many of these are in the hands of small owners, known locally as *malletos*. They personally cultivate the vines and carry out all the necessary treatments. It is claimed that the vineyards of Sanlúcar are the best looked-after in the whole sherry region and this must help with the quality of the wine they produce.

There have been two comparatively recent developments that have helped producers to satisfy the rapid increase in demand for manzanilla. One of these has taken place in the vineyards; the other in the wineries. All books on sherry talk of the three types of soil that are found in the vineyards, the *albarizas*, the *barros* and the *arenas*.

Historically, vineyards were planted on all three, with the finest wines coming from the albariza, or chalk-based soil. It is interesting that if you drive through the heartland of the area, the *Jerez Superior*, in winter the contrast between the white of the chalk vineyards on the summits of the rolling hills and the barros, or clay soils, at the bottom is striking. The big advantage of the chalky soils is that they retain water well. In the sherry region, the rain falls mainly in February, March and April, with the summers being totally dry. This means that for the vine to thrive it must be able to draw on the reserves stored within the sub-soil and here it is the chalky soils that are supreme.

The barros soils are coarser and give high yields of inferior wine. The arenas, or sandy soils are the poorest of all and were widely planted at the time of phylloxera, because they provided the vine-shoots with some protection.

As with many other wine-producing regions in the world, the major problem has been to strike a balance between supply and demand. As far as sherry is concerned, the situation is exacerbated because, by law, the wine must have a minimum average age of three years. The use of the word 'average' in the legislation makes the law very difficult to apply and this has been achieved by insisting that no company can sell more than a third of its stock in a year. This demands intelligent forward planning. Whilst the domestic demand for sherry has remained comparatively stable, production has to be led by export sales, which account for three-quarters of the total. During the 1950's and 60's, these increased rapidly, reaching a peak in 1979. To satisfy this demand, there were extensive vineyard plantings, often on barros and arenas soils. Between 1970 and 1982, the area under vines had increased by 87%.

Then sales suffered a vicious decline. In 1983, there was an initial four-year plan, which called for the distillation of vast quantities of surplus wine, a halt in the planting of vineyards and the grubbing up, within one year, of a tenth of the vineyard area. Whilst the policy was fine, its implementation was largely non-existent.

By 1989 the crisis had become so severe that the Regional Government of Andalucia commissioned a report from the international firm of accountants, Price Waterhouse. Amongst their recommendations was that the area under vines should be reduced by a further 5,200 hectares, later cut down to a compromise figure of 4,000 hectares. Naturally this reduction mainly applied to those vineyards, often quite recently planted, on more marginal soils. These have since been planted with alternative crops such as wheat, sugar-beet and sunflowers, enabling further surplus mountains and lakes to be created! The one undoubted success from all this is that most sherry grapes are now grown on the finest albariza soils; the production of manzanilla demands grapes of such quality. This is the first important change that has taken place.

At the beginning of the nineteenth century, there were as many as forty-three different grape varieties listed as being grown in the sherry vineyards. Now this figure has been reduced to approximately ten, of which only three have any significance: the palomino, the pedro ximenez and the moscatel. The first accounts for 90% of the total plantings and the other two are used for the production of sweet wines. For manzanilla, only the palomino is now used, though even in such a comparatively small area as that of Jerez, it has hidden under a number of aliases, such as listán, tempranilla, palomina blanca and orgazuela.

48

The palomino is a strange variety, for it shows itself at its best either as a table-grape or in fortified wines, particularly when it has been influenced by flor. Elsewhere in Spain, it has been planted in Rueda, where it accounts for 19% of the plantings, and is used in the production of *vinos generosos*, the largely neglected historical speciality of the region. It is also found in León and Galicia, where it is prized for its large yield. It is also grown in Australia, South Africa and California, where it has been produced for the local 'sherries' or for the most basic 'jug' wines. In the South of France some is grown under the name of Listán, where its neutrality is often masked by judicious blending with such varieties as chardonnay.

The second important change has come at the stage of fermentation. When Manuel González Gordon wrote in 1948, "Different sherry musts, although made from a single variety of grape, grown in the same soil, even in the same vineyard, and harvested and pressed the same day, may, on fermentation, produce completely different types of wine, even if the fermentation has taken place under identical conditions," he was only reporting the situation as he saw it at that time. Until then, fermentation had invariable taken place in oak butts of 30 arrobas, or, alternatively, and very rarely, in earthenware *tinajas*. It was almost a matter of chance whether the resultant wine would turn out as suitable for selection for turning into fino or oloroso sherry.

Because of a shortage of oak for the making of these butts, experiments were carried out with fermenting the musts in tanks lined with glass tiles. Whilst these were much easier to clean, it was found that cracks developed in, or between, the tiles, which could harbour undesirable acetic ferments. As a result of further experimentation, it was discovered that concrete vats, painted on the interior, were more suitable, particularly if temperatures could be controlled at the time of fermentation. Nowadays, almost without exception, fermentation takes place in stainless steel vats, where temperature control can be total. Now wine destined for fino or manzanilla can be produced on demand. Without this, it would have been impossible to satisfy the resulting demand from a change in consumer preference. We now have the perfect juice for turning into sherry; it is at the fermentation stage that the 'sex' of the sherry – fino or oloroso – is determined.

What distinguishes the production of sherry and manzanilla from that of any other wine is what is known as the criaderas and solera system, which is sometimes described in English as a 'fractional blending' system. This original method has as its final result a wine which does not belong to one particular vintage, but rather one which comes from a mix of vintages. In your glass you find elements of wine which may be no more than three years old but also of wine that might be a hundred or more years old. This results in the wine having a continuity of style and taste over the years.

As has been mentioned already, the key to the production of manzanilla is the process of ageing. This consists of putting the wine in casks made of American oak, known as butts. The casks are then grouped together in lots, each one of which will have wine of a different age. These lots are known as *criaderas* or *clases*. These lots of butts remain in a fixed place in the warehouse, or bodegas; so it is the wine that moves round and not the casks. The final *clase*, in which the wine reaches its peak of maturity, and from which a proportion is drawn off for bottling, is known as the solera. This generally has been from the lowest rows of casks, closest to the ground and this is how it has achieved its name – from *suelo*, the Spanish word for ground.

In the warehouse the butts are generally stacked three or four high, and when some of the wine has been drawn off from the solera for bottling, the resultant void in the casks is replenished with wine from the first criadera, which in its turn is replenished from the second criadera and so on. It is the fact that only a small proportion of the contents is drawn from each cask on each occasion, that gives continuity of style to the ultimate wine.

One of the distinctive features of the creation of manzanilla is that the wine might pass through as many as 14 to 16 criaderas, whereas these are much fewer in the production of other styles of sherry.

Generally speaking, wine is taken from the solera for bottling at least three times a year. This leads to an advance through all the criaderas of all the wines in the system. As can be imagined this is very time consuming and labour intensive. This 'general post' is known as a *saca*.

Nowadays, the transfer between the butts is carried out with multi-piped pumps, each of the pipes going to an individual cask. The wine which is taken out from the different butts in a clase is pumped into a tank where it is mixed together before being pumped in to the butts of the next clase. Formerly all this work used to be done by hand, with the cellarman transferring the wine from one cask to another in large jugs, or *jarras*.

The result of this continuous blending is a wine that comes, not from an individual vintage, but from a combination of many vintages. Occasionally, and it is indeed very rare, a wine may be made and aged separately from a single year, but this is a risky and hazardous step.

The butt is the standard unit of measurement for the cellarman and it has a capacity of 511 litres or 108 imperial gallons. The ideal wood for these is well-aged American oak, for this transfers no extraneous flavours to the wine. In the warehouses, the bottom rows of butts are placed on bases, either carved out of rock or made from concrete, called *bajetes*. Between the bottom of the butts and this base is a thin layer of cork and a mat of esparto grass.

Second-hand sherry butts have long been the casks of preference for the ageing of Scotch Whisky. This was particularly the case when sherry was shipped in cask to England for bottling. Now that bottling has to take place within the sherry region itself, butts are used much less frequently. However, there are certain distilleries that finance the purchase of butts in Spain and then lend them to sherry companies so that they can absorb the essence of the wine. In practice, second-hand Bourbon barrels are more regularly used, for, under American law, that whiskey has to be aged in new barrels.

When the butts are re-filled, this is not to the brim, but a gap is left – this is particularly important in the production of manzanilla.

Manzanilla, fino and amontillado (this last sherry is the child of one of the other two) form the fino family and are produced from *yema*, or must, that comes from the free-run juice of the grapes, which falls by gravity, after a gentle pressing. The three develop as a result of a biological ageing, which is influenced by a particular natural enhancer, flor.

No-one knows for sure how the solera and criadera system came about, but it may well be because the unsold wine of one vintage was mixed with that of the following vintage and this blending activated flor for the first time. It was the Arabs who added alcohol to wine in order to make it more stable for shipment to far-off markets. The addition of alcohol and the presence of flor both played key roles in the evolution of the solera and criadera syatem.

Flor consists of a mixture of bacteria and spores of the *saccharomyces* family which form a film on top of the surface of the sherry in the casks. It is not that the flor imposes itself upon the wine, but rather that it generates spontaneously from the bacteria present in the air and on the ground. It can play its role naturally solely on wines within the narrow range of 14.5° and 16° alcohol, so it does not occur on the heavier wines that develop into olorosos.

In the sherry region flor is an active sugar-consuming yeast and, by covering the surface of the wine, acts as a barrier between the wine and the air, thus minimising oxidation. In the hotter, drier climate of Jerez, the flor is particularly active during the spring and the autumn, whilst in Sanlúcar, where the climate is more influenced by the Atlantic Ocean and is, as a result, cooler, it is active throughout the year. That is why, in Sanlúcar, the bodegas are all constructed so as best to funnel in the sea breezes. Here the flor gives added protection and minimal oxidation.

Typically, up to four different fungi of the genus *saccharomyces* might appear in sherry flor; in Sanlúcar it is just one, *cheriensis*, that predominates. Sherry is by no means the only flor wine. It appears also in Montilla, Huelva and Rueda in Spain and in the production of *vins jaunes* of the Jura region in France. Notwithstanding such opposition, one local producer claimed to me that manzanilla "is the optimum expression of a flor wine".

This, then, is the key difference between manzanilla and the other wines of the region and what gives the town of

Sanlúcar exclusive rights to its production. The result is that if you have wines produced from the same grape, the palomino, from the same vineyard, with the young wine aged by the same solera and criaderas system in Jerez and Sanlúcar, which are just twenty kilometres apart, you have two different wines, fino and manzanilla.

One other vital difference is that manzanilla demands many more stages, or criaderas, in its production. It is as if the flor of manzanilla demands more frequent refreshment with young wine. The result is an ultra-dry wine, that is rather lighter in style than its relatives from the same region. To sum up: this is an easy to drink wine which is a pale straw in colour. The taste of something between saltiness and bitterness that has been bestowed upon manzanilla, comes about through the sea breezes which play such an important role in its creation. In a *copita* of manzanilla, you find the smells of seaweed and iodine concentrated.

Those other wines that are based on manzanilla, such as a manzanilla amontillada, also reflect this characteristic, but in a lighter way. Generally speaking, sherries produced in Sanlúcar share this *manzanillero* character, or are at least different in style to those produced elsewhere, in the sense that they tend to be more delicate.

We have talked about how whilst it is ageing in cask, manzanilla is protected from oxidation. However, once it is bottled, this protection no longer exists, and it can lose its big attractions, notably freshness and fragrance. In an ideal world, the wine should not be bottled until the order is received and it should be drunk as soon as possible after purchase. Indeed, two brands, La Guita and La Gitana, now have on their labels 'best before' dates.

Manzanilla is proud of its distinctive image, but it is not

just the wine that is different. It also has its own glass. In Jerez, you drink your fino from a copita; in Sanlúcar you will take it from a *caña*; rather than being of tulip shape, this resembles a small tumbler, indented at the bottom. The word caña is also used for something else that is distinctive in the cellars of Sanlúcar. This is the local *venencia* or tool used to take samples from the butt through the bung-hole. In Jerez, this is a tubular metallic cup at the end of a long, flexible handle traditionally made of whalebone, but now more often of fibreglass. In Sanlúcar this implement is rigid and made out of bamboo.

Mention has already been made of the important role that the bodega and its design plays in the ageing of manzanillas, but it must be stressed that there are two distinct styles of bodega in the town of Sanlúcar de Barrameda. These might be described as **acquired** and **constructed**.

During the eighteenth century Sanlúcar had become an ecclesiastical centre of some importance, with thirty-four religious establishments within the town, supporting almost five hundred priests, monks and nuns. With the dissolution of the religious orders by the President of the National Council, Juan Alvarez y Mendizabal, in the 1830's a vast number of urban buildings came on the market and many of these were bought by the newly emerging merchants in the wine trade. Thus, for example, Herederos de Argüeso now stores some of its wines in the sixteenth century refectory of what used to be the Convent of Santo Domingo. Such warehouses have had to be adapted for the ageing of wine and, one assumes, are often used for oloroso sherries, if they cannot meet the more demanding needs of manzanillas.

In some ways, then, Sanlúcar is similar to the Burgundian

wine capital of Beaune, where, after the French Revolution, many of the church properties were bought by the *négociants*, who were coming to dominate the local wine trade. However, whilst in Beaune it was not until the end of the twentieth century that purpose-built wineries came to be constructed outside the walls of the town, in Sanlúcar two 'colonies' of bodegas sprang up, one in the high town and one in the low town in the 1870's and 80's.

The first of these 'wine cathedrals', as they came to be called, was that of San Luis in the Barrio Bajo, however the most impressive one of all is that of La Arbolelilla in the Barrio Alto. This was built in 1876 by Cipriano Terán Carrera, with the aid of his site foreman El Conejito – 'the little rabbit'; one can only wonder how he gained this nickname!

This enormous bodega is 118 metres long and 33 metres wide. The central pillars are ten metres tall and the roof's heigh is 12.5 metres at its apex. Absolutely no metal was used in its construction and so that it could benefit to the maximum from the sea breezes, it points 23° east of north. It now stores the wines of Antonio Barbadillo.

For the perfect maturation of manzanilla, the ideal characteristics of the bodega have been laid down for us by Isidro García del Barrio Ambrosy:

> **"Temperature**: *There should be minimum changes in temperature between day and night and througout the year. At cask level it must not exceed C25° and should not fall below C12°.*
>
> **Humidity**: *Similarly, this should be as constant as possible between day and night and throughout the year. It should be as high as possible, with no upper limit. The relative humidity should remain*

above 50%.

Aeration*: Must be as high as possible as flor relies on air. By its nature it is aerobic.*

Other requirements*: Minimum light, noise, vibration and smells.*

To create this ideal, the bodega will be constructed so as to minimise the effects of the sun and to maximise those of the sea breezes. It will be painted white on the outside to reflect the heat. The roof will be of hollow Arab tiles over a layer of coarse bricks. These provide effective insulation. The floor should be of earth, composed of yellow sand and lime. This helps considerably with humidity. The walls should be at least 60 centimetres thick, and should be made of such material as rubble, which again provides effective insulation and assists with the internal humidity. The windows are oblong, rather than rectangular, to prevent the sun's rays entering. They also have heavy wooden latticed shutters, again to minimise the effects of the sun, whilst, at the same time, permitting currents of air. These windows are carefully placed high in the walls to cut out the effect of the levante east wind, while encouraging the humidity brought in by the westerlies. Finally, again to minimise the effect of the heat, there should be neither windows nor doors in south-facing walls."

These were the recommendations of Garcia del Barrio in 1979 for the construction of the ideal maturation warehouse for manzanilla. Doubtless modern techniques have introduced alternative methods of achieving the ideal humidity, temperature and aeration. In addition, there are two further essentials for producing good manzanilla. Firstly, you need good base wine and, secondly, you need the native flor. Out of the gross overproduction of sherry at a time of falling demand came the decision to uproot much of the area under vines. As has already been said, the lesser vineyards planted on barros and arenas soils were the first to go. This has meant that the proportion of grapes suitable for the production of the more elegant manzanilla (and fino, for that matter) has risen considerably. In addition, the rapid advances made in vinification techniques, and this is particularly important in such a hot climate, have enabled the transformation of healthier must into better base wines. Without these parallel achievements, there would have been no way of satisfying the rapid increase of demand for manzanilla that has transformed the domestic market and is now slowly conquering those overseas.

It is said that flor suddenly appeared in the sherry region at the end of the eighteenth century. Over the years, it is the Sanluqueños who have best succeeded in developing the methods of encouraging its growth, and its year-round activity that gives the wines of the town their distinctive difference. Whilst the wine might have come about as a result of an accident, it is now the lifeblood of the town and it is a heritage that is guarded proudly and, on occasion, fiercely. This inheritance is tied up in the buildings that not only house the wine, but also play a major role in the creation of their individuality.

There are, however, other factors that make manzanilla stand out from the sherry pack. One of these is the way that the solera system is applied. Again, there is little evidence as to when this form of fractional blending was adopted in the region, though it is widely believed that it was first used in Sanlúcar. In Jerez, the norm is between five and eight scales in the solera, in Sanlúcar there are often twice as many of these. For example, San León, the manzanilla of Argüeso, has an average age of ten years and passes through eighteen stages in the criadera. The great sherry expert, Manuel González Gordon, has suggested the more stages there are in the criadera, the better it is for the wine, "The reason for this is that the extensive aeration produced has an extremely favourable effect on the maturing process."

As has been seen, oak butts play an essential role in the creation of all sherries. They are the nests in which the eggs are hatched. These casks are made of what is known as New Orleans oak, which has a rather coarser grain than French oak which is preferred for the maturation of many wines. Many sherry butts are extremely old – a hundred years or more – and every sherry house will employ coopers to maintain them. Sanlúcar is one town where the art of the cooper is appreciated and still thriving.

Whilst manzanilla is a member of the sherry family, it prides itself on its independence; an independence that it has earned from the distinctive features of its production. Whether a manzanillla is better than a fino, may be a matter of taste, but there is a distinction and this distinction owes part to the Atlantic Ocean, part to a fungus and part to the time and care that go into its creation.

Where Manzanilla Stands in the Sherry World

What is understood by the term The Sherry Zone is the geo-graphical region accepted for the production of wines under the *Denominaciónes de Origen* (D.O.s) for Sherry/Jerez/Xérès and Manzanilla. This is loosely bound in by the three towns of Sanlúcar de Barrameda, Jerez de la Frontera and Puerto de Santa Maria, or, to put it another way in an imaginary triangle with these towns at the angles that form it, with the Atlantic Ocean as its south-west hypoteneuse.

According to the prescriptions laid down by these D.O.s, all the different types of sherry can be produced from vines anywhere in the region. (Peculiarly, for the production of sweet wines, it is also permitted to bring in pedro ximenez grapes and wine from Montilla and Malaga.) As far as manzanilla is concerned, whilst the grapes can come from anywhere in the zone, the wine must be developed and aged within the limits of the township of Sanlúcar de Barrameda. Every bottle of manzanilla has to provide evidence of its upbringing to receive the authentification of the authority that controls the D.O.s, the Consejo Regulador. As a result of this, limits are imposed on the production of manzanilla, that apply to no other wines produced within the zone. To put it another way, this makes manzanilla the most exclusive wine produced in the region.

There is no general agreement as to whether manzanilla is just another type of sherry or whether it is a distinct wine in its own right, with a separate character. Whatever may be the reply to this question, it is important that it is not ignored, for, in the first case, if it is just another sherry, it is an exclusive sherry, with a distinct background and upbringing, as demanded by law.

Recent statistics show that it is the most widely drunk sherry – if we accept the first case – or wine from the sherry zone – if we accept the second – in Spain. On the other hand, as far as foreign markets are concerned, until recently manzanilla has been the great unknown of the sherry family, for the preference has generally been for cream, or sweet, wines.

We have seen how, following a peak in consumption in Spain, and particularly in Andalucia, during the nineteenth and the beginning of the twentieth centuries, manzanilla was replaced by fino in the glasses of the consumers. During this period of absenteeism, the wine merchants of

Sanlúcar existed by selling their wines in bulk to the merchants in Jerez, who were enjoying a golden era. They achieved record export figures at the end of the 70s. This led to commercial activity in Sanlúcar being, for most, no more than passive. There was only a handful of companies which tried to sell products under their own brands in the domestic market. Nevertheless, at the beginning of the 80s, a decline began in orders from the sherry houses of Jerez. This, in its turn, forced the Sanlúcar companies to become more active in the market and to introduce manzanilla once more. This led to an upswing in sales.

A prime example of this change in consumption patterns is the city of Seville. Historically it used to receive daily supplies of manzanilla in cask, shipped overnight up the Guadalquivir, but with the economic expansion of the 60s it had become an important consumer for fino. Now there was a major change; manzanilla, under its individual brandnames, became the call. The *feria* of Seville is the greatest annual occasion in the world where sherry is drunk. Fino was forgotten; manzanilla was on everybody's lips … and down their throats. Manzanilla was reborn.

What are the causes of this sea-change? The first reason is that consumers have been seeking out lighter wines. This change in taste was foreseen as early as 1972, by Manuel González Gordon in his book *Sherry, the Noble Wine*. This is becoming increasingly more noticeable; the search for wines with less alcohol, colour and sugar, wines more acceptable to doctors and to diets. Out of the sherry family, manzanilla is the wine that best fits this bill.

The better standard of living and education in Spain has led to the consumer having a greater knowledge of wine and being more able to appreciate individual styles. This, in its turn, has led to more specialisation. Here again, manzanilla has benefited as it is the most individual wine in the region and the one with the most restricted production.

The Socialist government which was in power for twelve years from 1982 brought a return to what had been popular and the fact that manzanilla is something both authentic and traditional from Andalucia meant that it was able to profit from this nostalgia. In the broader world the fashionable image of both Spain and Andalucia meant that there was increased interest in this individual wine.

In spite of all these favourable circumstances, the renaissance of manzanilla is mainly due to its inherent quality as a wine. This is born out by the tastings that regularly occur in the specialist consumer magazines: manzanilla generally stands out and receives markings above the average.

It might also be said that manzanilla is a food-friendly wine. With increased interest in gastronomy at all levels, it has managed to establish itself in the minds of the consumer as a sherry, as a wine, that can be drunk with food. One has only to see the amount consumed in the restaurants of Bajo de Guía in Sanlúcar to gain an idea as to how popular it might become. With the increasing fashion for tapas bars around the world, there is no better accompaniment than a bottle of manzanilla.

Indeed, until now, most manzanilla has been consumed in Spain on traditional occasions such as at fairs or on pilgrimage. By its nature, this restricts sales and the producers are now making great efforts to promote it as a light wine that goes so well with seafood, such as the prawns for which Sanlúcar is also noted. Whilst Guinness is the traditional liquid of choice at the Galway Oyster Festival, manzanilla would be just as fitting a partner!

Improvements in techniques of vinification and stabilisation have enabled the manzanilla producers to guarantee quality after bottling. Just as an apple tastes at its best when eaten straight from a tree in the orchard, so does manzanilla taste best when freshly drawn from the cask in the bodega. Modern treatments of filtration and stabilisation now mean that a bottle of manzanilla opened in a bar in Stockholm tastes just the same as one opened in a bar on the Plaza del Cabildo in Sanlúcar – that is if both come from the same bottling run and have been well kept.

Once a bottle has been opened and, in the unlikely circumstances, that it has not been finished, it can be kept in a refrigerator without the quality suffering. As an aside, in Andalucia the fashion is to order manzanilla by the half-bottle, a readily consumable quantity. Would it not be a good idea to promote this form of consumption more widely? Manzanilla by the glass might lead to bars stocking opened bottles in less than ideal conditions, with a resultant suffering in the quality, and the reputation of the wine.

On a global basis, manzanilla ranks no higher than number four in sales of the various categories of sherry. However in Spain it has more than half of the market and it is the only category which has maintained or increased its sales over recent years. Whilst the sales of *vinos generosos* have tumbled, manzanilla has gained market share.

It is interesting that there had always been a feeling amongst sherry *aficionados* in Britain that the finos and manzanillas that they enjoyed in Spain were more elegant and lower in alcohol than those available here. It was believed that alcohol was added to make them better able to travel. This has been demonstrated to be a myth, by the fact that sales have continued to increase in Britain and

Germany, where it is now permitted to import the wine at 15°. Now the full attraction of the wine has been revealed to us. Now the same wine can be enjoyed anywhere in the world.

(A further result of this reduction in the strength of manzanillas and finos is that there has been an almost total collapse in the sales of the wines of Montilla, which had enjoyed a certain following because they had not suffered from the necessity to ship at above 15°.)

Whilst manzanilla has a history of which it can be proud, it must also look to the future. The world of wine becomes more competitive by the day, but manzanilla has an individuality that no other wine can claim. If it is to build on its current resurgence, it needs to flaunt its charms around the world and turn its faithful followers into ambassadors. Fairs and pilgrimages may provide solid foundations, but a large and stable house is not going to be built on them. Manzanilla must promote itself as a modern wine for modern people.

The Wine People of Sanlúcar

So far we have looked at the way that the wine, manzanilla, is produced, but now it is time to look at the people and the companies that are involved in its production.

As has already been explained, the base wine for the production of manzanilla can come from anywhere within the sherry region. However much of this does, in effect, come from vineyards within Sanlúcar such as Miraflores. It is a surprising fact that vineyard holdings in the town are much more fragmented than anywhere else in the sherry zone. Research, carried out in the year 2000, shows that whilst the vineyards of Sanlúcar represent no more than 12.54% of the total area under vines in the D.O., the number of individual vineyard holdings represents 29.01% of the total and the number of owners 28.78%. To put it more graphically, the average size of a vineyard holding within the boundaries of the town of Jerez de la Frontera is 12.15 hectares, whilst in Sanlúcar it is no more than 1.19 hectares. The vineyards of Jerez cover just over 6,700 hectares and there are 430 owners; those of Sanlúcar, just over 1,300 hectares, but there are 810 owners. This, then, is a town of small peasant farmers, rather than of large sherry houses.

For the grower, there are three main possible outlets for his grapes. Firstly, he can sell them directly to one of the large producing companies, and this may not be in Sanlúcar; it might just as well be in Jerez, though this might present transportation problems and with the high temperatures at vintage time it is wise to get your grapes to the press-house as soon as possible. Secondly, he might be a member of one of the local co-operative cellars, and there are two of them in the town. Because of the number of small growers, their role is perhaps more important here than elsewhere in the region. The third possibility is that the vineyard proprietor might also be an *almacenista*. That is to say he will make the wine himself and store it in his cellars, where he might have his own criaderas of limited size. He will then sell the finished wine to the merchants. Historically, there were many almacenistas, some of notable size, in the town, who would provide a vital source for the base wine for Jerez finos. However, with the increasing popularity of, and demand for manzanilla, many have created their own brands and have a dual approach to the market. As we shall see, the number of pure almacenistas is now comparatively small.

Let us look then at these various organisations and in addition, some of the other sherry houses, particularly in

Jerez, that sell important quantities of manzanilla. For whilst the production of the wine is strictly limited to the town of Sanlúcar, is sales and distribution have a much broader base.

HEREDEROS DE ARGÜESO S.A.

The Argüeso family has long been at the heart of the production of manzanilla, for not only did it own the company that was established in 1822, but it is related by marriage to the Hidalgo family, and also one of the leading almacenistas is an Argüeso. However, Sanlúcar is only a small town and marriages between the sherry families are more the rule than the exception!

The founder of the company, Leon de Argüeso y Argüeso arrived in Sanlúcar from Arija in the northern province of Burgos, no doubt attracted by the burgeoning export trade in the wines of Andalucia. Indeed, he began his life there provisioning ships and it was some years before he bought some existing cellars, with their stocks and the vineyards to back them up. One of the properties that he bought, in around 1840, was the former Taberna del Reloj (Clock Tavern) and high on the building that now stands on the site, there is a sundial to commemorate this. Part of his investment was in existing soleras, so the company is able to claim that it has stocks, however infinitesimal, that predate its foundation.

Don Leon remained a bachelor all his life, and, on his death, bequeathed the company to his nephew and niece Juan and Francisca. These are the heirs referred to in the company's title and are remembered in the company's trade-mark, which incorporates a bottle labelled J y F, surrounded by LOS 2, in large print.

The company has three bodegas in the centre of the low town; the main one, with offices in calle Mar. This accounts for two-thirds of their storage space. The two other smaller ones are in the nearby calle Trasbolsa. The dispatch warehouse is in what used to be the refectory of the sixteenth century Dominican convent. In total they have 15,000 butts of ageing wine. They used to have a sixty-hectare vineyard, Poedo, on prime albariza soil, as the major source for their wines, but this was sold recently by the Argüeso family to the present owner of Bodegas Barón. However, they do have long-term contracts with growers who own a further 230 hectares. In 1992, they opened a new vinification plant outside the town on the road to Chipiona.

Whilst the company sells a million and a half bottles of sherry a year, of which 80% is manzanilla, it maintains a low profile, though it does claim to be the market leader in the Province of Seville. Until recently no more than 8% of their sales were in export markets, though they now claim that this has risen to 30%. Another important reason for their restricted recognition is that they have always played an important role as almacenistas for other sherry houses, supplying them with their manzanilla requirements in bulk. Indeed, the company has long enjoyed a high reputation for the age and quality of its wines. Witness is borne to this by the fact that many of the local bars in Sanlúcar offer it as their house wine of preference, often directly from the cask.

Commercially, the company has manzanilla brands at three different levels. The youngest wine is the Manzanilla Fina Argüeso, which has seven stages of criadera. Then comes Las Medallas de Argüeso, which is also a manzanilla fina, which has eleven stages and an average age of five years. Finally comes their most important brand San León, with an average age of ten years and eighteen stages. As their promotional literature boldly proclaims: "This is not a manzanilla for everybody, but there is no doubt that it is the most widely appreciated by those who know anything about wine." However it is a wine whose style has been somewhat lightened over the years.

This is a company that has great potential, for it has perhaps the most important stocks of old wine in Sanlúcar. Like many of its competitors it was family owned, with the result that there were too many shareholders pulling in different directions. This created difficulties when it came to creating a forward-looking commercial strategy. As a result, the family sold out in 2006 to a company in the field of property investment. Whilst they have stated that it is their intention to continue to expand the company, one fears that their investment may have something to do with the town-centre sites that the company owns. Argüeso has been one of the quality leaders in the field of manzanilla, let us hope that it continues long to be so.

ANTONIO BARBADILLO S.A.

To place the Barbadillo family in perspective within the broad picture that is Sanlúcar is not easy, for, in many ways they dominate the town. Of all the companies here, they are by far the largest sellers of sherry, though, interestingly, not of manzanilla. The Dutch wine writer, Hubrecht Duijker, says that they own 70% of the total wine warehouse space in the town. Various members of the family have written books of local history and of their family, as well an anthology of poems praising the local wines. In addition, the company has been public-spirited enough to publish facsimile editions of earlier books of interest to vinous historians. (Good use has been made of the facility in the creation of this book.) On top of all this, the company has created the first wine museum in the area in an eighteenth century house close to the Castillo de Santiago. The Barbadillos come at you from all sides!

The earliest mention of the family, which appears to have originated in the town of Covarrubias, in the Province of Burgos, dates back as far as the tenth century, when they were involved in a terrible story of revenge killings, worthy of a Greek tragedy. What began as an argument at a wedding party, ended up with the contract killing, by a group of Moors, of seven brothers. This deed is still commemorated in the family coat of arms.

The wine history of the family, however, begins with Benigno Barbadillo, who, at the age of seventeen, followed his uncle, a priest, to Mexico where he appears to have made his fortune. After twenty-four years in the Americas, he returned to Spain, via London, in 1821. He soon established himself in the wine trade and purchased a bodega. At that time Sanlúcar was a centre for the production of *vino de color* and business appears to have boomed from the beginning. Amongst his early customers are such famous sherry names as Osborne, Rivero and Duff Gordon.

Wine did not represent his sole business interests, for the archives include an invoice for a cargo of wheat, shipped from Seville to Cartagena, in present-day Colombia. By 1826 he was sending wine to London and, in the following year, manzanilla is mentioned for the first time in an invoice for wine sent to Philadelphia, which included *"Jerez Superior, Pajarete seco y abocado, Moscatel, Dulce Blanco y Dulce de Color."* It is not until three years later, that manzanilla appears again, this time in an order sent to Jersey, seemingly an important market for him. Interestingly, amontillado is not mentioned until as late as 1840.

Don Benigno died in 1837, leaving five young children and the company in the hands of his widow. She, perhaps to bring future stability to the firm, married the company accountant, Pedro Rodriguez, in 1840. In due course the name of the company became Pedro Rodriguez e Hijo, with Pedro owning 75% of the shares and Manuel Barbadillo the other 25%. Sr. Rodriguez proved a more than competent successor and an astute businessman, greatly increasing the value and standing of the company. He was the first person to launch a bottled manzanilla, Pastora, and he obtained the warrant to supply the Spanish royal family. Vizetelly includes a description of a visit to the company at that time in his book on sherry.

Antonio Barbadillo, who is remembered in the current name of the company, was born in 1863, the grandson of Don Benigno. He married into one of the leading local wine families, the Terans, and under him there was a rapid expansion in the sales of bottled wine, with the creation of new manzanilla brands, such as Eva and Sirena.He greatly increased the company holdings in vineyards, bodegas and, most important of all, in stocks of wine.

He died in 1921 and further expansion of the company followed immediately after the Spanish Civil War. There was much planting of vineyards, of which they came to own almost 150 hectares, a very considerable holding at that time. The Second World War saw three separate moves with regard to sherry, none of which helped the merchants of Sanlúcar. First of all, in 1942, the price for grapes grown on albariza soil reached a new peak, up 40% on those of the previous harvest. Secondly, total sherry exports collapsed from 76,000 butts in 1940, to 44,000 butts in 1941. Thirdly, there was a dramatic increase in the sales of Jerez brandy, up by an enormous 37% in a single year in 1940. This led to a relative strengthening of the role of the more solid merchant houses in Jerez de la Frontera and Puerto de Santa Maria, vis à vis their Cinderella sister in Sanlúcar. It was in the aftermath of all this that that the Rumasa group was able to establish itself in the world of sherry (not to mention banking and the hotel industry) for there were many skeletal companies on which the vulture could prey. The resultant house-of-cards empire was based on such weak foundations and the ability to shuffle paper between its various affiliated companies in three continents. The ultimate collapse of this group had two results for Barbadillo, one of them beneficial, the other costly.

The Showering brothers, who had made their fortune from the creation of Babycham, a sparkling and mildly alcoholic drink made from pear juice, that in no way, apart from its name and the glasses that were created for drinking it, resembled champagne, purchased the venerable Bristol wine merchants John Harvey & Son Ltd. They had two particularly valuable assets: the first was a royal warrant as wine merchants and the second was the registered trade-mark for one of their sherries, Bristol Cream. This had rapidly become a major world-wide brand and the rights, somewhat surprisingly, as sole suppliers of the sherries in the blend had been granted to the Ruiz-Mateos family, of Rumasa. Harvey's came to see that they had made an error and terminated the contract, for a substantial indemnity, which fuelled the ever more rapid expansion of Rumasa. Barbadillo received their first order for a thousand butts of wine, as new suppliers, on the Day of the Three Kings (Twelfth Night) 1966. This is a major feast-day in Spain, and the day, rather than Christmas, when it is traditional to give and receive gifts!

This was just the first of many orders, leading to Harvey's purchasing 10% of the capital of Barbadillo. (This has since been bought back.) More importantly there was a substantial new investment in the planting of new vineyards and the construction of an ultra-modern new vinification plant. In all 1,400 hectares of land were purchased at Gibalbin, to the north-east of Jerez and 1,000 of these were planted with vines. This is where all the Barbadillo wines are now vinified. It is with some justification that the company proudly painted on the wall of one of their bodegas, BARBADILLO PROVEEDORES DE HARVEY OF BRISTOL. (Barbadillo suppliers of Harveys of Bristol.)

The second investment that Barbadillo made as a result of the fire-sale of the collapsed Rumasa empire, had less happy consequences. A decision was taken in 1988 to buy Williams & Humbert, a company founded in 1877 and whose most successful brand, particularly on the American market, was Dry Sack. As Antonio Barbadillo wrote in the 2nd edition of his book, *Historia de las Bodegas Barbadillo*, which was published in 1993, "I dedicated chapter five of the first edition of this book to Williams & Humbert, saying that 'I cannot omit a reference to this bodega, because, whilst for us it is not history, it is very much the present.' As far as the second edition is con-

cerned, it is now history, and a very short one at that."
Subsequently Williams & Humbert has been sold to the
Dutch group Ahold and the Spanish Medina group.

As well as the joint venture with John Harvey, Barbadillo
owns a further 250 hectares of vines, the Viña Santa Lucia,
on the road from El Cuervo to Arcos de la Frontera. Between
them, these properties supply 60% of the company's needs,
the balance being made up by purchases of must.

It should be pointed out that as well as producing 200,000
cases of manzanilla and 125,000 cases of other sherries each
year, the company is responsible for Spain's top-selling white
table wine, Castillo de San Diego, made from the palomino
grape. Surprisingly, exports account for no more than 40%
of their turnover and 80% of this is sherry sold under the
customer's own label. They recognise the need to build up
awareness of their name in overseas markets.

The top selling manzanillla brand of Barbadillo is Solear,
which has reidentified itself as a manzanilla fina, having traditionally been a manzanilla pasada. Their brand Muy Fina,
which is somewhat lower in price has a particular following at
local fairs. A more specialized wine is their manzanilla en
Rama, of which they bottle a small quantity into half-bottles
twice a year. This is bottled straight from the cask with minimum treatment. The label specifies the year and season of
bottling. The suggestion is that the wine should be drunk
before the end of the season of bottling. A proportion of the
sale price is donated towards supporting wild-life projects,
particularly in the Coto Doñana National Park. (This idea is
based on an original concept of Javier Hidalgo of Bodegas
Hidalgo – La Gitana, where part of the sale price of a bottle of
old palo cortado, was given to support the protection of the
imperial eagle.) Other manzanilla brands that they currently

offer on the market include Eva, Mil Pesetas and La Pastora.

The company's head office is situated in the Casa de la Cilla, which was originally built in 1773, as a centre for the collection of Episcopal tithes. Nevertheless, it played this role for a comparatively short time in its career; tithes being abolished in 1841. The company purchased it in 1939. It has a beautiful colonnaded courtyard and a magnificent staircase. The company holds stock in thirteen different bodegas, in both the high and low towns. The biggest of these is the Arboledilla, truly a cathedral of wine. After the collapse of the Rumasa group this passed through a number of hands, before being purchased by Barbadillo from the Hidalgo company.

There is no doubt that Barbadillo is the biggest fish in the pond that is Sanlúcar, but in the vast ocean that is sherry, it is brands that count and here it has been left far behind by its big brothers in Jerez. In a bid to diversify its business interests it has recently purchased vineyards and a winery in the Ribera del Duero and Somontano D.O. areas and a Spanish company selling premium quality hams from 10,000 free-range pigs roaming the forests north of Seville. Like many of its direct competitors in the world of manzanilla, it is a family company, with a broad number of shareholders. Elsewhere, this has often led to unhappy solutions.

BODEGAS BARÓN S.A.

History is important in the wine trade and whilst this company, founded in 1871, is not amongst the oldest in Sanlúcar, it claims ten generations of wine experience. The founder, Manuel Baron Fernandez married Dolores

Romero Sanchez, from the Romero de la Balsa family, who had owned vineyards in Sanlúcar since the middle of the seventeenth century. When the company was formed, it purchased the very old soleras of the almacenista Anselmo Paz and these soleras still provide the base for the best wines of the company.

The company owns its own vineyards, split now between three sites, the Finca Atalaya, the Finca Martin-Miguel and the recently-purchased Poedo. Whilst the company owns a number of bodegas, the manzanilla criaderas are in the Bodega de los Molinillos, which was purpose built in 1871. In all, they own approximately 10,000 butts of wine.

The new owner of the company, a local entrepreneur, has recognised the danger in being no more than a stock-holder for the major companies of Jerez and has sought to develop sales under his own brands. Whilst the company offers the complete range of sherries, it is, quite naturally, proudest of its manzanillas. These include, in ascending order of price: manzanilla Fina Baron, Micaela, Atalaya and Solera San José. At present, exports account for no more than 10% of their turnover.

C.A.Y.D.S.A.
(Criadores, Almacenistas y Distribuidores de Vinos de Jerez S.A.)

The origins of this company date back to the end of the 18th and the beginnings of the 19th centuries, when it was founded by an immigrant from Genoa called Esteban Bozzano. In its initial form, it was a company that dealt in textiles, but swiftly moved into wine under the direction of his son Francisco, who additionally built a distillery, which mainly distilled spirit from the pomace of the pressed grapes. (The tiled chimney of this distillery can still be seen in the high town.)

It was his son, also called Esteban, who expanded the wine business and purchased two bodegas San Luis and Santa Ana, named after their former owners. On his death, the company passed into the hands of his widow and was known as Viuda de Esteban Bozzano until 1969. It was one of many medium-sized companies operating in the wine trade and in a 1919 list of employers in the sherry trade in Sanlúcar, it came ninth, below such companies as Hidalgo, Gonzalez Byass, Argüeso and Barbadillo, but above Delgado Zuleta, Rainera Pérez Marín and Pedro Romero.

By 1969, the company had fallen on hard times. Its stocks had run down, its debts had run up and it had exhausted its credit with the banks. The owners went to their competitors seeking help. Shortly before, there had been established a buying group known as BUSA (Bodegas Unidas S.A.) jointly owned by a number of bodegas including Barbadillo, Hidalgo and Argüeso. Their first operation was to buy a sawmill, which made wooden shipping cases for the wines. The shareholders in BUSA bought what was left of Bozzano and the vehicle they used for this was a new company called CAYDSA.

The company was furnished with stocks and a successful sales network established, not just in Spain, but also in export markets. Sadly, however, there was a disagreement amongst the shareholders and they, in turn, sold it in 1980 to the main co-operative cellar in Sanlúcar, the Cooperativa del Campo Virgen de la Caridad. As this cellar had been responsible for supplying much of the sherry for the recreation of the company, this proved to be a satisfactory outcome for what might have turned into an unseemly row between some of the main families in the local wine industry.

Almost a thousand growers were the shareholders in CAYDSA and sent their grapes there for vinification. The cellar is very traditional and was perhaps the last in town to ferment its musts in earthenware *tinajas*, as are still used in the production of Montilla – and in certain other wine regions of Spain. Naturally, it is much more difficult to control fermentation temperatures in such vessels than in what is now the ubiquitous stainless steel.

Because of the nature of the company, it plays a more important role as a supplier of young wines in bulk to the merchants and almacenistas, than it does as a producer and distributor of branded manzanilla in bottle. However its manzanilla fina Bajo de Guía is widely seen in the local bars, as is, on a lesser scale, their manzanilla pasada la Sanluqueña.

In the autumn of 2009, there was a development in the life of this company; it was purchased by Nueva Rumasa, the new revelation of the Ruiz-Mateos family. It will be interesting to see in which direction this will lead them.

LA CIGARRERA

Any visitor to Sanlúcar soon becomes aware of this company, for there are signs around the town inviting tourists to come and taste, and presumably also buy, their wines in their bodegas. However the company is something more than just a tasting cellar, as its origins go back to 1758, when Joseph Colom Darbo arrived from Barcelona and established himself in the town. An 1873 guidebook to Sanlúcar by Jose Rosetty, mentions two members of the family as having active trading interests in the town. The company is now run by the Hidalgo Garcia de Velasco brothers, who are the ninth generation in direct succession from the original founder.

Like many similar companies, for most of its existence it has acted as no more than an almacenista, but in 1998 it decided also to sell its wine, originally just manzanilla, in bottle under the brand name La Cigarrera, with a label that could well be a promotional poster for the opera Carmen. Since then other sherries have been added to broaden the range, which now sells not just at the cellar-door, but throughout Spain and, to a very limited extent, in certain export markets. It is also seen widely in the local bars as a 'draught' manzanilla sold by the glass.

Whilst, historically, the company had its own vineyards, these have been sold and it now sources its young wines from local growers and co-operative cellars.

COVISAN

This acronym stands for the Cooperativa del Campo de Viticultores de Sanlúcar, the smaller of the two cooperative cellars in the town. It was founded in 1968 to give a number of local growers readier access to the market. At present there are something over two hundred members, who are the shareholders in what is now a limited company. The small average size of the individual holdings can be seen from the fact that between them they control the production of just 235 hectares of vines.

The cellar has twelve hundred butts for ageing wine, as well as stainless steel tanks for fermentation. It has recently installed a bottling-line and its wines are being distributed both locally and nationally by the second-level co-operative group AECOVI, based in Jerez. Their manzanilla is being sold with the brand name Mira la Mar.

DELGADO ZULETA S.A.

In the world of wine, there is probably no other town that has as high a proportion of historical, family-owned companies, as Sanlúcar. Delgado Zuleta is yet another one of these and, in fact, pre-dates all its competitors. It was established in 1744 by the Honorary Mayor of Sanlúcar, Don Francisco Gil de Ledesma, Knight of the Order of Calatrava. (This military and monastic order, perhaps the most prestigious in Spain, was founded in the twelfth century to defend the town of the same name against the Moors.) The current name was adopted by the company at the end of the nineteenth century and the shares are now owned by more than a hundred members of the same family.

The company's wines enjoyed particular favour when the royal family established its summer home in the town. One regal story is of King Alfonso XIII, the last king of Spain before the dictatorship, toasting the crew of one of his submarines as it lay submerged off the north coast of Spain. The wine chosen was their La Goya.

In 1978 they merged with Rodriguez Lacave, a company originally founded in the eighteenth century by a French merchant living in Sanlúcar. Many of the Rodriguez family remain as shareholders.

The company primarily relied on the fifty-hectare vineyard, Viñas Dolores Nudi, part of the Miraflores pago, for their grapes. This vineyard was separately owned from Delgado Zuleta – but had the same shareholders, who sold it in 2009. Further requirements are met by long-term contracts with individual growers.

At one time the company owned as many as fourteen different warehouses around the town, but this number has now been reduced to eight; even this must present certain logistical problems, perhaps more so because the head office is situated just outside the town on the road to Chipiona. Their oldest cellars are in the Casa de Indios, a reminder of the time when the town was the main Spanish port for trade with the West Indies and the Empire in the Americas.

This is a company that is very much oriented towards selling manzanilla. Of its total annual sherry sales of 150,000 cases, no less than 74% is of this style. The criadera supporting their leading brand, La Goya was first laid down approximately a hundred years ago. In style it is a manzanilla pasada and is named in honour of Aurora Joffre, a leading flamenco dancer at the time of the First World War, and whose stage name was La Goya.

Delgado Zuleta claims that La Goya is the top-selling brand in Sanlúcar iself, and also in the neighbouring town of Trebujena. To satisfy those whose taste is for a manzanilla fina, they offer the brand Zuleta and a third string to their bow is a brand they inherited from Lacave, Barbiana. Historical brands which still have a certain following are La Galvana and Lola.

Because of the size of its stocks, it has also played an important parallel role in the manzanilla trade as an almacenista, selling wine in bulk to other sherry houses and also to local bars for consumption by the glass.

Delgado Zuleta is a company that recognises that it needs to expand its sales beyond the traditional local markets. Currently exports represent no more than 16% of their turnover, but their wines can be seen in limited quantities in North American and some European markets. The wines are of high quality and deserve further exposure, yet, in the world of sherries, the necessary promotional budgets may be beyond their resources. This is a pity for those consumers who enjoy quality traditional manzanillas.

J. FERRIS M

Sr. Jesus Ferris Marhuenda and his wife were owners of important vineyard holdings on the road from Sanlúcar south along the Atlantic coast. In 1975 they built their own bodegas, with a capacity of 10,000 butts, "situated between El Puerto de Santa Maria and Sanlúcar de Barrameda, where the quality is best for the finos of Jerez and the manzanillas of Sanlúcar." On the death of Sr. Ferris and his wife, the company was inherited by three of their children, who now run it. They have a full range of sherries, including two manzanilla brands Piconera and La Liebre. In addition they have a range of red table wines including the rare, and sweet, Tintilla de Rota.

GASPAR FLORIDO S.A.

The Florido family has a long and proud history in the sherry trade. They trace their wine interests back to a Martin

Florido who lived in Rota in the sixteenth century. At the end of the seventeenth century, the family moved to Chipiona, but they appear to have finally taken the decision to establish themselves as merchants in 1800 when Jose Maria Florido y Calderon de la Barca began trading. In 1880, the company became Florido Hermanos and rapidly developed into an outift of some substance, at peak ranking among the top ten exporters of Jerez. This company was ultimately purchased by Pedro Domecq.

It was the father of the current Sr. Florido who re-established the company in 1942 and for many years it acted solely as almacenistas selling wine in bulk. Indeed, it was only in 1997 that they were 'forced' into selling wine in bottle under their own label.

Members of the family own thirty-three hectares of prime vineyards in the Miraflores pago, Viña Armijo, where they also own a beautiful sixteenth century house. The wines that they sell in bottle all come from their own vineyards. Indeed, some of them are labelled Viña Armijo. However, they also buy must and wine for the bulk of their business. Historically, they had five bodegas spread around the town, but they seem to have centralised their stockholding of 7,000 butts in premises on the avenue leading out to Trebujena. As for their offices, unless you know exactly where they are, you may well spend time searching for them as they do not believe in advertising their presence with anything so normal as a sign!

One gains the impression that the biggest compliment that you can pay Señor Florido is to describe him as Conservative, with a capital C! Two of his favourite dicta are, "We maintain all the traditional methods; we have not adopted the modern bad habits", and "Cask wine is healthy, bottled wine is tubercular". He maintains that the finest manzanillas come from cellars on the south side of the hill of Sanlúcar, which are protected from the Levante wind and which have higher humidity.

Their manzanillas are drawn off unfiltered from the butts and sold in 5-litre containers to the local bars, but their despised wines in bottle are sold under the brands GF and Pleamar. In addition they offer such rarities as a manzanilla Olorosa en rama and a fifty-year old manzanilla Pasada Palo Cortado. This last wine is concentrated extract of manzanilla. Whilst they sell small quantities of wine in Germany, they are much more interested in selling in the domestic market, because of its ease of approach and the lower costs involved. They describe their work as *artesanía absoluta*, but, nevertheless, have been clever enough to register for themselves the websites jerezsherry.com and manzanillasanlúcar.com!

Sadly, events have overtaken Sr. Gaspar Florido. Finding himself with no heirs interested in taking on the succession, he has sold the company to Pedro Romero S.A.

BODEGAS HIDALGO – LA GITANA

When the throne of Spain became vacant in 1759, on the death of Ferdinand VI, the successor was Charles, King of Naples and Sicily, a leading member of the Bourbon family. One of his first moves was to strengthen his new kingdom both culturally and economically. He was soon aware that the importance of Andalucia as a province had receded and he determined to restore it to its former commercial glory. As part of this campaign he encouraged immigration from the north of the country and it was because of this that Jose Pantaleon Hidalgo left his birth town of Casteñeda, in the province of Santander, and came to settle in Sanlúcar de Barrameda. Here he bought a small bodega from a local businessman Roque Verjano and married his daughter. It was their son, Don Eduardo Hidalgo Verjano, who created the company that is now known as Bodegas Hidalgo – La Gitana, for it was he who planted the vineyards and built the bodegas that are the foundations upon which the company has grown.

Don Eduardo was fortunate to live at a time when not only the wine trade was booming, but also the town of Sanlúcar itself. It was around this time that commerce was encouraged by the wide availability of property due to ecclesiastical disestablishment. With this there came a rapid expansion in a prosperous middle class. Further impetus was given by the decision of the Monpensier branch of the royal family to build their summer house in the town. This naturally attracted a number of court followers.

Don Eduardo was very active in municipal affairs and was one of the promoters of the Jerez – Sanlúcar – Bonanza railway, which was constructed in 1877. (One of the results of this was that some land that the Hidalgo family had bought at the farmhouse of the Casa Alta, was expropriated.) This involvement in public life led to Don Eduardo being granted the title of Marquess of Pagollano – a title he declined to use because of his 'liberal' political leanings.

From the beginning, the company prospered and we see that, during the Peninsular War, it seized the opportunity to sell to both sides, a feat that is commemorated in its existing labels: an old amontillado being called Napoleon and an old palo cortado, Wellington.

T.G.Shaw, writing in 1864, speaking of an un-named bodega, says: "Sherries were shown to me, in one great bodega, for a butt of which it was declared (how truly I know not) that £1,000 would not be taken. It is not for a moment pretended that the wine is worth any such money, but it is valued as a curiosity and ornament to the bodegas, as a painting may be to a dining room. It has, however, a very substantial value, because the addition of even four or five gallons of such sherry to ten butts of very fine wine, worth £100, may so greatly improve them that each will bear the charge of £120.

"These wonderful wines are known as the Napoleons, because it is stated that when the first Emperor Napoleon was in Spain, in 1808 or 1809, he honoured the wine and the proprietor by condescending to approve a butt of this description, as his soldiers did of the less *recherché* kinds by drinking them all up! This, by the by, is an awkward historical fact against the reputed ages of some of these wines. But even in 1844 there was a long interval since Napoleon's visit; and there could not be a moment's doubt of the great age and original fine quality of some of them."

It is not clear whether the house of Hidalgo laid claim to the exclusive rights to the name Napoleon for some of its better sherries, or whether it became a generic term in the region, but it appears to be the only company laying title to the name nowadays.

Henry Vizetelly, another leading writer on wine, whose visit to the sherry region has already been mentioned, included a detailed study of the Hidalgo company in his *Facts About Sherry*, which was published in 1876. He wrote, "Señor Hidalgo, one of the principal growers of San Lucar and the largest holder of manzanillas, including the finest qualities of this delicate, aromatic wine, has, in addition to 1,000 butts of *vino de color*, usually stored in his bodegas no less than 5,000 butts of manzanilla, divided into fifteen soleras in various stages of progressive development, from the pale, fresh-tasting, and remarkably fragrant young growths, to wines in their fifth and sixth year, and regarded in fine condition for drinking, including also a wine ten years of age, accorded a medal for progress (sic!) at the Vienna Exhibition, with older wines which, although manzanillas, had developed much of the olorose and amontillado character belonging to the Jerez growths.

"Señor Hidalgo's wines are all the produce of his own vineyards, the most important of which, Miraflores la Baja, occupies some slopes a few miles distant from San Lucar, and yields 300 butts of manzanilla annually. Another vineyard in the same direction is Aquila, whilst a third in the neighbourhood of Chipiona, a little seaside village lying between San Lucar and Rota, goes by the name of Santo Domingo."

Don Eduardo died in 1889 and the following year his widow, Maria Josefa Luisa Colom y Gutierrez, created a new company Viuda y Hijos de E. Hidalgo. It is interesting to look in the archives and see an inventory made the following year. There were three separate sources of income for the family: wines, farms and salt-pans. There were five separate vineyards: the Viña Miraflores of 78¼ *aranzadas* (an aranzada is an historic Spanish measurement approximating to 1 acre, or 0.4 of a hectare), Viña El Alamo (52 aranzadas), Viña El Cuadrado (44¼ aranzadas), Viña El Amarguillo (7½ aranzadas) and Viñ Santo Domingo of 126 aranzadas, but this also included arable land, palms and 100 olive trees in addition to the vines. There were seven separate bodegas;

the main one, together with the commercial offices, being on the Plaza Victoria.

The stocks of wine included the famous Jerez Napoleon, as well as Pedro Ximénez and a Moscatel Viejisimo, which was valued seven times as much per litre. They also held important stocks of sherry vinegar and lesser ones of brandy. More surprisingly there were also casks of Madeira and Malaga. They also held small stocks of sherry 'on consignment' in both London and Liverpool. Amongst their agricultural inventory was a five-year-old bull, called Montenegro, who lived on the salt-marshes.

Only two years later, one of Don Eduardo's sons, Jose Hidalgo Colom, broke away from his mother to establish a company called J. Hidalgo y Cia. In due course he was followed by other of his brothers, who went their own way and established what was to become Hijos de Rainera Pérez Marín, with adjoining bodegas. This company is now the producer of La Guita sherry. The parent company rapidly disavowed the sons and renamed itself Viuda de E.Hidalgo, which over the years metamorphosed into Vinicola Hidalgo and, more lately, Bodegas Hidalgo La Gitana. (In no way should it be confused with the Jerez company, Emilio Hidalgo; a mere upstart, founded in 1874.) It is now the sixth and seventh generations of the Hidalgo family, in direct succession, who are managing the company, largely with the same vineyards and the same bodegas.

During the Spanish Civil War, many European warships patrolled the Straits of Gibraltar, to protect their shipping and the interests of their nationals living in Spain, as well as, in the case of Germany and Italy to provide military support. No shore-leave for the sailors seems to have occurred without a visit to a bodega, and the Hidalgo visitors' book is full of inscriptions from thankful sailors. Amongst the more interesting is one dated February 2nd 1937, after a visit from the crew of the *Graf Spee*, famous in British naval history for the role that it played in the Battle of the River Plate. The one on this occasion finishes, "... and when you come to this friendly company, I am sure that you will go away drunk". signed, Jupp Schehr.

Like most companies in Sanlúcar, the primary historical role of Hidalgo has been that of an almacenista. That is to say it has produced sherries from its own vineyards, has aged them and then sold them in bulk, either to the major wine houses in Jerez, or abroad for bottling under the label of the customer. Where this company has been fortunate is that it has created for itself a brand with widespread recognition, firstly in Andalucia, where it really counts, and then further afield in other parts of Spain, and then in foreign markets. It is frightening to think that almost eight bottles of manzanilla sold out every case of twelve, do not go beyond the boundaries of the province of Seville – and that approximately a third of those are consumed in just one week at the Seville fair. It is in this narrow heartland of time and space that Hidalgo has conquered with its leading manzanilla brand, La Gitana.

Named in memory of an anonymous gypsy girl, whose original portrait still hangs in the company offices (is there any truth in the suggestion that she might have been a close friend of an historical member of the family?), this brand has developed, like so many others, from being a manzanilla pasada, into being a manzanilla fina and is now, in style, one of the lightest sherries on the market. On average it is approximately five years old and passes through fourteen stages in the criadera. In 2002, the very traditional presentation was changed to a more modern style, with a waisted, dark-green bottle.

Whilst La Gitana is by far the most important product in the company's portfolio, this does include two manzanillas pasadas, one of which, Pastrana, a single-vineyard wine from within the pago Miraflores, is building up a certain cult following for itself.

The company has its offices and its main bodega right in the centre of the town of Sanlúcar, on the Banda de la Playa. This name recalls the time, right up to the eighteenth century when this was the sea front. It also has two other bodegas in the low town, for the company believes the closer the warehouses are to sea level, the higher the humidity is throughout the year and this helps create the healthier flor, that is essential for fine manzanillas.

The company has its vinification centre, now fully equipped with temperature-controlled stainless steel vats, on top of a hill in the middle of its El Cuadrado vineyard (part of the Balbaina pago) on the main road to Jerez from Sanlúcar. The company owns 150 hectares of vineyards in its own right and is supplied by further vineyard holdings belonging to individual members of the Hidalgo family. All these vineyards are in the prime albariza pagos of Miraflores, lying close to the sea, due south of Sanlúcar, and Balbaina, south-east of the town, on the way to Jerez.

The company is still very much run by members of the Hidalgo family, among whom Javier Hidalgo has been particularly responsible for introducing the wines to foreign markets. Having trained as a biologist and as an agricultural engineer, he shares his love for manzanillla with that for horses and birds. He is one of the Trustees of the Doñana National Park and a board member of the Spanish Ornithological

Society that was founded by his father Luis E. Hidalgo Gibaja in 1954. He is also a keen amateur jockey – gentleman rider – making regular appearances at the famous race meetings in Sanlúcar, which take place each August.

Whilst Hidalgo may have spent the first two centuries of its existence in gentle expansion, it is now well aware of the great potential of manzanilla and has been at the forefront of campaigns for its promotion in both the United States and Great Britain.

BODEGAS INFANTES DE ORLEANS-BORBÓN S.A.

The Monpensier name is one of the most noble in French history and it is of interest to note that at least two Duchesses bearing that name took to the barricades in times of insurrection; namely Catherine Marie of Lorraine in the sixteenth century and Anne Marie of Orléans in the 17th. However, the history of this sherry house begins somewhat later with Antoine Marie Philippe of Orléans, Duc de Monpensier. In 1846, his father, Louis-Philippe I of France, made him marry, for political reasons, Marie-Louise de Bourbon, the sister of Isabel, the queen of Spain. Two years later, because of his liberal political leanings, he fell out with his father and moved to Seville, shortly afterwards taking up Spanish nationality.

In Spain, his politics also caused trouble for him and, at varying times, he was exiled to the Balearic Islands and Portugal. In the meantime, however, he had established a summer home for his family in Sanlúcar. At that time the wines of the town were very much in fashion and, in 1852 he purchased the Finca el Botanico, where he planted some vines. Eight years later he bought another property, Finca Torre Breva, which at that time was a shooting estate. This, too, he planted with vines, with the help of the latest steam-plough, imported from Ransome of Ipswich.

As has already been mentioned, we are fortunate that the development of this vineyard has been recorded for us by Henry Vizetelly, when he was researching his book on sherry. He visited the property at vintage time. As he wrote: "The most extensive vineyards at St. Lucar are those of Torre Breva, the property of the Duc de Montpensier, but now rented by an Englishman, Mr. R. Davies, one of the large Jerez sherry shippers. They are distant a long league from the town, and a drive bordered by fir-trees conducts through the plantation of vines to the house, distinguished by a tall square tower at one end. Here are no less the 320 acres of vines, no more than 200 of which are, however, bearing at present." He gives the yield of that vintage, low because of drought conditions, as being "upwards of 700 butts of wine". The vintage took sixteen days and the team of pickers and cellar-workers numbered two hundred and fourteen. Each day they consumed 360 lbs. of bread and during the vintage, enough grapes were eaten, that would have given more than twelve casks of wine!

In 1870 the Duke was an unsuccessful candidate for the throne of Spain, but on December 29th 1894, his son-in-law was proclaimed king as Alfonso XII. The family, therefore, became the leading one in Spain. It was not, however, until during the Second World War, that the grandson of the Monpensiers, the heir to the Spanish throne, created the commercial company. It is perhaps untrue to say that it was the grandson who created the company, for his main interests lay with flying. It was his wife Beatrice of Saxe-Coburg, who recognised the commercial potential of a range of sherries under their name. Thus it came about that the company was established in 1943, with the help of the Barbadillo company.

Initially, sales took off in the Spanish domestic market and exports soon followed. A particularly good agent was found in Holland, the Carp family, and a joint company was envisaged between the royal family, the Carps and the Barbadillos. Sadly, Mr. Carp died during the course of the negotiations and the agreement collapsed. Currently the vineyards belong to the Companía Agrícola Torrebreva S.A., which remains in family hands. This now produces table grapes in addition to those for the production of wine. The wine production and distribution company belongs half to the family and half to Bodegas Barbadillo, though the latter are responsible for both management and sales.

The main bodega is located in what used to be the Monpensier family stables where a full range of sherries is produced including two manzanillas Torre Breva and La Ballena.

HIJOS DE RAINERA PÉREZ MARÍN S.A.

In general, the world of sherry is not fast moving, but this is a company that has, in the past few years, expanded dramatically, largely on the back of a unique claim: "The only winery in the Jerez region that breeds, bottles and markets a single product – manzanilla La Guita".

The company was originally founded in 1852 by yet another immigrant from the north of Spain, Domingo Pérez

Marín, a native of Santander. He was a hard businessman and insisted in being paid by his customers in cash. In Andalucia, *guita* is slang for cash and this was at the origin of the brand-name. However, the word, from the same Latin roots as guitar, also means string, so, as a play upon this every bottle has a piece of string stretching from the neck to the body-label.

The bodega of Sr. Marín was yet another one that Vizetelly visited during his grand tour of the sherry region. An important moment in the company's history was when, at the beginning of the last century, some of the sons of Don Eduardo Hidalgo abandoned their widowed mother to build up Rainera Pérez Marín. They had their bodegas adjoining the family ones in the heart of Sanlúcar and Javier Hidalgo remembers when he used to go through a green wrought-iron gate in the communicating wall, to have breakfast with his aunt. The gate is still there but it was sealed up when the Rainera bodegas were, in due course, sold to be converted into a block of modern flats.

Recently, quite by chance, there came into our possession a price-list, dated 1967 from the London wine merchant Asher Storey. This company specialised in importing what were, at the time, lesser-known wines and the detailed notes were written by Gerald Asher, now a well-reputed wine writer, based in the United States. One of his rarities was La Guita and of it he wrote: "Sherry is essentially a blended wine, its origin usually lost in a complexity of vineyards and casks. La Guita is different and exclusive in this respect. It is a single vineyard wine coming from 150 acres of palomino vines owned by the Hidalgo family at Sanlúcar de Barrameda. No outside wine is allowed into it, and any wine from the vineyard which falls below the high standard set by the family is sold to the shippers' bodegas at Jerez or Puerto de Santa María.

La Guita, manzanilla pasada, *bottled in Spain* 23/-."

Since then, much has changed. The Hidalgo cousins sold the company in the 1970s and in 1990 it was bought by four former executives from the Rumasa group. Five years previously they had bought the small Jerez-based company M. Gil Luque, and they were seeking to expand their wine interests. In the meantime, the company vineyards in the Miraflores pago had also been sold, so the new owners needed rapidly to establish guaranteed alternative sources of supply. In order to achieve this, they astutely bought out the Miraflores Growers' Co-operative. This means that they have the exclusive rights to purchase the grapes from one hundred growers owning 150 hectares of vines in Miraflores – the same area from the same pago as the company had previously owned.

Another, more recent, development has been a change of style. La Guita is no longer the manzanilla pasada of Gerald Asher's time, but is now, as is the majority of its competitors, a manzanilla fina. The company, now the lynch-pin of the José Estevez group, owns four bodegas in Sanlúcar itself, of which the most important, in its previous guise, was the Hospital of Compassion of the Brotherhood of St. John, in the heart of the old town. Between them these warehouses are the home to 15,000 butts. They also have a fermentation cellar with a capacity of three million litres. The wine passes through a criadera of ten stages and is an average of five years old when it appears on the market.

In horse-racing terms, La Guita might be described as an unfancied outsider, who has left it late to come though on the outside to overtake the field. In the past few years, annual sales have increased from 50,000 cases to over 250,000 and its exports, to over thirty-five different countries, have doubled, as a proportion of sales to 30%. In Spain, it claims that Nielsen figures show that it sells more than the next two brands combined. Perhaps this goes to prove how successful just concentrating on a single product can be.

BODEGAS PEDRO ROMERO S.A.

The earliest claim to fame of the Romero family is that in 1740 it provided an outstanding bullfighter from Ronda. From there, they seem to have moved to Huelva, to the west of Seville, where they became distillers, mainly supplying spirit for the fortification of wines. In about 1820 Florencia Romero moved to Sanlúcar and married a local girl Agueda Carranza. It was their son, Vicente, who entered the wine trade in 1840 by buying an existing bodega and its stock, on the calle Trasbolsa in the low town, which remains their address to this day. The company was initially established as Vicente Romero Carranza in about 1860.

Initially the company specialised in selling brandies, particularly to the Spanish possessions in the Caribbean, especially Cuba and Puerto Rico, where their brand Pedro I was number two on the market. This brand has now been replaced by one called Punto Azul – and the name has an interesting background. Casks in the sherry region are made from American oak, but whilst most companies use what is known as New Orleans oak, those used for Pedro Romero butts come from Costa Rica. In that country apparently, the timber merchants mark the very best staves with a blue spot – *punto azul*. When Fidel Castro came to power in Cuba, he was still keen that their brandy should be available there, but that, in a bid to support the local sugar industry, it should be blended with cane spirit. As a security measure, therefore, they sealed the bungs of their casks with a blue seal – *punto azul*.

The three sons of Vicente: Vicente Jnr, Baldomero and Pedro came into the company at a boom time for manzanillas in the 1890s and began to develop sherry sales in parallel to those of brandy. (Whilst it has not received a specific mention in this book, brandy remains an important product for a number of local companies.) In 1904, Pedro bought out his brothers and named his top quality manzanilla Aurora, in honour of his wife. (This seems more politic than naming wines after gypsies or flamenco dancers, as his competitors had done.) He died in 1911 and his widow continued to run the business. However, this must have become increasingly difficult for her as a substantial holding in the company was sold in 1920. Notwithstanding this, the company is run completely autonomously with the Romero family still deeply involved. Indeed the current chairman is Santiago Romero, a Seville lawyer.

At one time the company owned a vineyard called El Alamo, though this has now been sold. Nevertheless, the name is still used by them as a brand for some of their sherries. They now buy their annual requirements as must from one of the co-operative cellars.

Whilst the chairman still considers the company's leading product to be his Punto Azul brandy, Aurora manzanilla comes a close second in his rating. This comes at two levels, the Aurora manzanilla Pasada Heritage and the Aurora

Prestige. This passes through 25 stages and its average age might be anything between nine and twelve years. Their manzanilla fina Pedro Romero averages five years old. Exceptionally, they have a manzanilla amontillado Don Pedro Romero Viejisimo Prestige, which is an average of forty years old. The size of this solera permits them to bottle no more than two butts a year of this wine.

There is an interesting contrast about the Pedro Romero company. In many ways it is the most traditional house in Sanlúcar. It does not hesitate to stick with the old ways of doing things; it claims to be the last company in the town to use fresh egg whites for fining the wines and the cellarmaster, Juan Bustamente, has worked for the company for more than fifty years. On the other hand there is a very young and ambitious board of directors. The main objective is to increase sales, particularly of sherry, not just in the domestic, but also in export markets. The latter have recently increased from a fifth of their turnover to about a third, whilst the former have been boosted by their supplying a full range of sherries to Carlos Serra, a major web-site supplier to the general public of Andalucian food and drink products.

To achieve this increase, without any sacrifice in quality, greater access to stocks of fine wine was needed and this has been achieved with the purchase of Bodegas Mendez, formerly Muller Ambrosy, and more recently Gaspar Florido, with its long established soleras.

The premises of Pedro Romero, between Bolsa and Trasbolsa streets, are well worth a visit, because condensed into one site, is the rich and varied vinous architecture of Sanlúcar, sheltering some twelve thousand butts of maturing sherry.

BODEGAS SAINZ DE BARANDA S.L.

This company was established some ninety-five years ago by a native of Santander, who set up a business in Sanlúcar as a general exporter. As a sideline a small sherry bodega and some vineyards were bought. Until very recently, it had been no more than an almacenista and it is only now that they have begun to sell bottled wine under the company brands Tia Cari, Paisana and Clarea.

Their bodega has a manzanilla pasada criadera of approximately 800 butts and their vineyard holdings now total about seven hectares in the pago El Hornillo.

MIGUEL SÁNCHEZ AYALA S.A.

This is yet another traditional Sanlúcar company that is moving from being a supplier of wine in bulk to the major shippers in Jerez, to selling bottled wine under its own brands. These include Gabriela and Las Cañas, as well as the long-established mark Pipiola, which was created by the now defunct house of Manuel Garcia Monge.

The company has an important vineyard estate of about 200 hectares, split between the pagos of Balbaina, Torre Breva and Martelilla. Its annual production is of about 5,000 hectolitres of sherry, of which approximately half is manzanilla.

In 1986, the company, together with all its stock, vineyards and brand names was bought by a local businessman, Jose Luis Barrero Jimenez.

The Almacenistas of Sanlúcar de Barrameda

In most wine-producing regions, trade is split between the growers and the merchants. As far as sherry is concerned, this is also true; most of the major brands are backed by substantial vineyard holdings. On the other hand, most of the independent growers are small and have joined one or other of the co-operative cellars in the region for the vinification and commercialisation of their wines or musts. However, there is also a third group of some importance in the sherry trade; that is the almacenistas.

Often an almacenista comes from one of the liberal professions. He may own vineyards, or he may buy must from a co-operative, but, sometimes as little more than a hobby, he will have his own bodega with one or more soleras of sherry. This wine he will sell in bulk to the shippers. Historically, some companies would only support a very limited range of their better-selling brands from their own stocks, whilst for the peripheral wines that they had on their price-lists, they would draw on those of one or more almacenistas with whom they might have a long-standing relationship. For example, whilst the companies of Sanlúcar quite logically promote their own manzanillas, they might have customers who demand a fino. Rather than maintain their own solera outside Sanlúcar, it is much easier for them to rely on the continuity of the solera of an almacenista in Jerez or Puerto de Santa Maria. The corollary has also been true. With the increasing demand, particularly in Spain, for manzanillas this has meant that Jerez-based companies have had to establish their own bodegas in Sanlúcar, or source their wines elsewhere in the town, either from one of the local companies or, alternatively, an almacenista. Some major Jerez companies, Gonzalez Byass for example, have long maintained bodegas in Sanlúcar, for the local wines have often been a vital part of their fino blends. Others, however, have always found it more practical, or more commercially viable, to rely on almacenistas.

The particular importance of this specialist in Sanlúcar is underlined by the fact that whilst almacenistas exist in all three sherry producing towns (the other two being Jerez de la Frontera and Puerto de Santa Maria), their numbers elsewhere are much lower. On the official register, there are seven cellars in this category in Jerez, two in Puerto and fifteen in Sanlúcar.

One Jerez company, Emilio Lustau, part of the Caballero group, has made a virtue of promoting the wines of individual almacenistas as higher-priced speciality quality wines, available only in strictly limited quantities. As far as manzanilla is concerned they feature wines from two soleras of Manuel Cuevas Jurado. Whilst this is an astute marketing ploy, it does not mean that the wines are any better because they come from an almacenista. It does imply, however, that the wines have a certain individuality – and rarity. Many of the major houses also offer such individual wines, more so perhaps now that the aged-related classifications have come in.

The boundaries between what is defined as a "Bodega de Crianza y Expedicion" and what is a "Bodega de Crianza y Almacenado" are somewhat blurred. As we have already seen, many that have traditionally been no more than almacenistas have taken their first faltering steps into the world of selling wine in bottle under their own label. At what stage does their category change? It might be said that there is little difference between bottling the wine yourself and selling it, or shipping in bulk to have it bottled by a company such as Lustau.

With middlemen being cut out in many aspects of the trade, it is not surprising that the role of the almacenista is coming under severe pressure and the co-operative cellars, which have been historically the almacenistas *par excellence*, are now creating their own brands and selling their wines directly, for fear of being squeezed out of the market. Other Sanlúcar companies, such as Sainz de Baranda and La Cigarrera have made the same move in the recent past. There is nothing new in this; the once mighty Rumasa group had its origins as a humble almacenista!

The official list of the "Bodegas de Crianza y de Almacenado", based in Sanlúcar is:

Agrícola Sanluqueña S.L.
Ángel del Río e Hijos S.L.
Bodegas del Sur S.L.
Bodegas Méndez S.L.
Carbajo Ruiz S.L.
Cooperativa Virgen de la Caridad
Elena Romero Lopez
Fernández de Argüeso C.B.
Francisco Yuste Brioso
Herederos de Rafael Terán C.B.
José Gálvez Rodríguez
Juan Carlos Pérez Rodríguez
Manuel de Argüeso Hortal
Mercedes Jiménez García
Maria Caridad Barbadillo García de Velasco

It is interesting to see such locally famous family names as Argüeso, Teran and Barbadillo on the list. Realistically speaking, there are a further eight or nine bodegas in the town whose role is primarily that of an almacenista.

Other Houses with Manzanilla Interests

Whilst, as has been made clear, manzanilla has to be aged in Sanlúcar de Barrameda, this does not prevent other companies, primarily those in Jerez, from having manzanillas in their portfolio. Indeed, there are Jerez companies that maintain bodegas in Sanlúcar. Here are three of the most important:

GONZALEZ BYASS Y CIA.

As has already been mentioned in previous chapters, since the 1980s there has been a dramatic change in the pattern of sherry drinking within Spain; manzanilla is now queen and fino has been relegated to second place. 1994 was the first year, in recent history, in which sales of manzanilla overtook those of its rival. Since then sales of the former have increased, though not always so rapidly, whilst sales of the latter have decreased. On world markets however, sales of both have fallen, though, in Britain for example, awareness and consumption of manzanilla seems to be widening. The pens of many writers seem to consider it as an individual wine in its own right, rather than as a sherry.

Tio Pepe, in the mind of many consumers, is synonymous with fino, and often in some remote corner of the world when you ask for a glass of sherry, you receive the reply, "Do you mean Tio Pepe, Sir?" This is the big brand of Gonzalez Byass and it would not be surprising if they had a somewhat ambivalent attitude towards manzanilla. They claim this not to be so and they foresaw a happy future for their own brand El Rocío, which, they pointed out, was only one of four wines from their stable to be repackaged at the same time as Tio Pepe. Notwithstanding this, at present the brand appears to have been withdrawn from the market. Could this be a case of *reculer pour mieux sauter?*

The success of Tio Pepe must largely be due to the reputation that it has enjoyed for its unvarying quality and it regularly comes out the winner in competitive tastings of dry sherries. One of the reasons, of course, is that it is backed up by unrivalled stocks in the Gonzalez bodegas. One other might be that it is rumoured that a high proportion of the blend that makes up this wine depends on base wines that come from Sanlúcar.

The connection between Gonzalez Byass and Sanlúcar is a long one. It begins in the year 1783, when, at the age of twenty-five, Jose Antonio Gonzalez, who had worked in the royal court, was appointed to the important post of *Visitor General de las Rentas del Reino de Sevilla* – effectively financial controller of the royal salt-pans of Sanlúcar, that had been established not long previously by Carlos III. At this time the town was enjoying a commercial renaissance, not just with the rapidly expanding wine trade, but also as a horticultural centre. The port also was very active in the West Indies trade.

He married a local woman, who bore him seven children. The fifth of these, born on May 25th 1812, was Manuel Maria Gonzalez. He was educated locally and gained his first commercial experience in the offices of a company of general traders in the town, Lasanta y Cia. Amongst the products that they handled was sherry and it was in this that Manuel saw his future.

At the age of twenty-three, he moved to Jerez, and with the help of his uncle, Tio Pepe (*tío* is the Spanish word for uncle) he entered the export trade as Bodega de Manuel Gonzalez. Two of his early partners, his uncle and Francisco Gutierrez Aguera, were also natives of Sanlúcar. However, there is no trace of his having specialised, or even sold, the wines of the town of his birth. He died in 1886 and it is probable that it was his son, Pedro Nolasco Gonzalez Gordon, who began selling the, then fashionable, manzanillas. The company purchased the existing Sanlúcar business of La Viuda de R. Majon, together with its stocks and brand names.

This company must have been of some substance, for, when Vizetelly visited its cellars he noted particularly the age and the quality of some of its wines. "We tasted in different bodegas scores of wines ranging from their first up to their ninth or tenth years, and found that it was only when the wine was in its fourth or fifth year that the peculiar bitter aromatic flavour for which manzanilla is distinguished had completely manifested itself. In Señora Manjon's bodega, we tasted manzanillas twenty years old. One of these wines had developed a distinct amontillado character, while another was of the nutty-flavoured oloroso type." At about the same time, the company appeared in a guide book to Cádiz and the region, as Sra. Viuda de Manjon, Pradillo, Doña Leona Mergelina.

We do not know whether the worthy widow had had her fill of commerce or whether the Gonzalez family paid a good price for stocks of old wines in her bodegas, however the labels under which she sold her wines are in the Gonzalez Byass archives. Amongst her brands were: manzanilla Canaveral de la Perla Fina, manzanilla Montañeses de la Perla Fina, manzanilla Las Monedas 'vinos criados al natural' and manzanilla Solar. Also included was the Leona amontillado Fina. These brands must have had a following for they continued to be used by Gonzalez Byass.

Alongside these Gonzalez Byass had its own brands: these included Piedra, used both for manzanilla fina and manzanilla pasada and Reina Mercedes. Interestingly, the company had two separate brands for manzanillas olorosas, and specimens of these labels still exist, both for exclusive importers in Montevideo, Uruguay. One of these brands was Mari Pepa, which, coincidentally, is now used for the cream sherry of the company Gutierrez Colosia.

Some idea of the importance of the company within the town of Sanlúcar can be gained from the list of shareholdings in the local mutual benefit society, founded in 1919. The number of shares issued to each company depended on the number of their employees – and Gonzalez Byass headed the list with Hidalgo.

Mention has already been made of their manzanilla brand El Rocío. The name commemorates Andalucia's most important local pilgrimage, to a spot at the northern edge of the Doñana National Park. It is not clear when the brand was first created, but the label was designed by a leading artist of the 30s, Carlos Gonzalez Ragel.

Another possible reason for the disappearance of a manzanilla from the Gonzalez Byass portfolio, could be their takeover of the bodegas and brands of Croft. With Croft Original Pale Cream, they now have a second leading export brand. Supporting these will need increased effort and investment, We can only hope that we will see once again evidence of the company's backing for quality manzanilla.

EMILIO LUSTAU

This company was founded in 1896 by Jose Ruiz-Berdejo to carry out the role of almacenista, supporting the major sherry houses. Some forty years later, the management was taken over by his son-in-law, an immigrant from France, who then gave the company its current name. Since then it has built up a solid reputation as a quality supplier. In every wine region there is a handful of producers repected by all their peers; in Jerez, Emilio Lustau is in that handful. Concerns were expressed, in 1991, when it was taken over by the Puerto de Santa Maria sherry company Luis Caballero, but these fears have been groundless; their autonomy and the quality of their wines have been maintained. Indeed, as we shall see their warehouse facilities have been considerably improved.

For many years, the reputation of Lustau was based on

their ability to provide excellent wines for the B.O.B. market – where sherries are sold not with the label of the supplier, but rather with that of the customer. In 1982, however, they took an innovative step which was to place their reputation on an even firmer footing; they launched a range of almacenista sherries. In the big branded world of sherries, this was the equivalent of offering a Fabergé easter egg in a high street jeweller's shop. The concept of promoting 'hand-crafted' sherries in limited (and often very limited) quantities, was one that had immediate appeal. For, example, a restaurant in the heart of rural Wales that I visited recently, proudly proclaims how fortunate it is to have a restricted range of these sherries available for its customers.

As has already been explained, in the world of almacenistas, Sanlúcar has a particularly important role to play. Whilst just a quarter of the total stock of sherry maturing in the region is within that town, somewhat over a half of that in almacenista cellars is there.

Because of the special relationship that Emilio Lustau has forged with the almacenistas, the company has created a particularly strong reputation for its manzanillas. In all they deal, on a regular basis, with as many as ten almacenistas in the town, but their closest relationship is with Manuel Cuevas Jurado, who combines business as a grocery wholesaler of some substance, together with the paying hobby of producing sherry. His wines come from his own albariza vineyards in the local La Callejuelas pago. Lustau features two of his wines, a manzanilla pasada de Sanlúcar, which comes from a solera of eighty butts, with the criaderas to support it and a manzanilla amontillada, from a smaller solera of just twenty-one butts. Both of these are outstanding wines. In addition, the company sells under its own label the Solera Reserva Papirusa manzanilla.

Historically Lustau had its cellars within the centre of the town of Jerez. Its offices were on the Plaza de El Cubo, built into the city walls. In 2001, however, it bought part of the former Harvey bodega, which, in its turn, had formerly belonged to the Marqués de Misa company. These have now been restored and the offices and cellars are on the same site. In all the company has stocks of some 15,000 butts.

In addition to relying on almacenistas, Lustau is support-ed by 170 hectares of vineyards in the Jerez Superior zone. One of these is La Cruz de Husillo, in the pago of Balbaina Alta. This was mentioned by Richard Ford in his book on travels in Spain in 1845.

There is no doubt that manzanillas are treated as an important part of the portfolio of Emilio Lustau. The fact that they export as much as 95% of their production has meant that the reputation of the wine has spread far and wide.

BODEGAS WILLIAMS & HUMBERT S.L.

For those who know their sherries, Williams & Humbert and manzanilla may appear unlikely partners and it is prob-ably fair to say that this has come about as the result of a marriage of convenience. However, there has been a slight connection between Sanlúcar and the company ever since its foundation. It was established in 1877 by Alexander Williams, who had worked in the offices of Wisdom & Warter in Jerez, and Edward Engelbach, who had been sent out by Coutts Bank in London, to administer the properties of the Monpensier family in Sanlúcar and elsewhere. The Engelbach participation in the firm only lasted ten years and what had been Williams, Engelbach & Co. became Williams & Humbert, with Arthur Humbert, the brother-in-law of Arthur Williams, as the new partner.

Half a century earlier than this, in 1821, a company called Viuda e Hijos de Perez Megia, was founded in Sanlúcar, with bodegas in the calle Fariñas. Over the years, it built up a reputation for its manzanilla Alegría and its manzanilla amontillada Jalifa. In the report of 1919, it was rated as the 14th largest wine company in the town, based on the number of its employees. At the end of the twentieth century, the company was absorbed by Luis Paez S.A., itself part of the Medina group, which had been established by the brothers José, Nicolas, Jesus and Angel Medina, who had established this sherry empire with the support of the Dutch multi-national, Ahold.

In the meantime, Williams & Humbert had passed through very difficult times. In 1972, it was absorbed as one of the jewels in the crown in the Ruiz-Mateos group and when this collapsed in 1983, most of the spoils were rapidly distributed to eager purchasers. However, José Maria Ruiz-Mateos claimed that the brand name Dry Sack belonged to him personally, and this chilled the eagerness of those interested in buying Williams & Humbert. The matter was finally resolved in an English court, and, as has already been mentioned, Antonio Barbadillo purchased a controlling interest. This proved to be an unhappy move for them and they sold the company on to the Medina group, the owners of Paez.

As a result of developments within the group, Alegría and Jalifa now stand alongside Dry Sack, Pando and A Winter's Tale, in the Williams & Humbert portfolio. Whilst the bulk of their production is based in a vast new facility, just outside Jerez, they maintain a bodega in Sanlúcar for ageing manzanilla. Here they warehouse 3,000 butts of wine to support annual sales of 50,000 cases of Alegría. This, they claim, makes it the fifth largest brand on the market. Backing this up is the wine from 350 hectares of prime albariza vineyards.

We must be grateful that one of the great historic brands has survived the many years of problems suffered by the original company, Perez Megia, and its successors.

OTHER MANZANILLA BRANDS

Whilst, over the years, a number of sherry houses have included a manzanilla within their portfolio, the resurgence of interest in the wine has led to a wider range of brands becoming available. Amongst these, here are some that have not already been mentioned:

La Caletera – Bodegas Almocaden, Jerez
Juncal – Bodegas Garvey, Jerez
La Rubia – Bodegas Valdivia, Jerez
Ria Pita – Dios Baco, Jerez
La Bota de manzanilla 'las Cañas' # 8 –Equipo Navazos, Jerez
Gutierrez Colosia, Puerto de Santa Maria
Cara de Gallo – Osborne y cia., Puerto de Santa Maria.
Viva la Pepa – Sanchez Romate Hermanos, Jerez
La Lidia – Vinícola Soto (Garvey), Jerez
Viña la Callejuela, Sanlúcar de Barrameda

The Gastronomy of Manzanilla

The wine of Sanlúcar is so versatile that we can approach its relationship with food from three different directions: as an aperitif, as an accompaniment to food and as a vital ingredient in certain recipes.

As a member of the sherry family, manzanilla has been best known as an aperitif, rather than anything else. In Spain itself, there are occasions when manzanilla is considered to be the aperitif *par excellence*. One of these, for example is the Seville Fería when thousands of people get together and drink 600,000 bottles of manzanilla within just six days. Here it might be accompanied by almost anything:

114

dried fruit, olives, potato crisps, or thick or thin soups and then charcuterie, shellfish, cheese, meat, fish – or whatsoever you fancy. During the Fair, aperitif time lasts the full twenty-four hours of the day, for there is little formal eating, but rather snacks on the hoof.

Another occasion when manzanilla might be considered as a prolonged aperitif is on one of the annual religious pilgrimages which are popular throughout Spain, but particularly in Andalucia. The most important of these is El Rocío, at Pentecost. Here a family group of thirty-five people might consume over a thousand bottles, during the eight days that it lasts. It will be offered freely to any who wish to come and share it. As at the Fair, manzanilla is drunk here with almost anything, eaten on foot or on horseback, during the dancing at any hour of the day or night.

In and around the town of its birth, it is drunk on a wide number of occasions, such as weddings, baptisms and private parties. At the race meetings in Sanlúcar it is the drink *de rigueur* to accompany the broad range of foods on offer.

It appears that the term tapas was first created at the beginning of the twentieth century when a member of a certain club in Seville asked the doorman to bring him his normal *cañero* of manzanilla, together with some slices of ham, from the bar next door. The barman placed the slices over the glass like a cover, *tapadera*, or tapa, and from that day on, the members of the club ordered their manzanilla in just that way, be it with ham or other snacks. Thus tapas owe their very existence to manzanilla. Nowadays tapas have diversified and almost anything to eat, taken in small portions, has adopted the name.

In earlier times, when stress scarcely existed and when people could devote more time to living, it was traditional to take tapas and an aperitif in a bar before lunch. Thus grandfather Pepe Argüeso used to spend a couple of hours every lunchtime on the journey between his office in the Argüeso bodega and his home. Both of these were in the town centre and the distance between them scarcely a kilometre. He used to stop in every bar on the way for a glass of manzanilla and a tapa. In such a way, he created the leading brand on the local market and exhausted the patience of his wife.

As a dry wine, with a certain body, manzanilla is well placed to accompany a wide range of dishes in a formal meal. Here it can play the role of a table wine.

In conservative circles in Sweden, as for example, on the great forestry estates, sherry is always served with soup and if the soup is of fish or shellfish, manzanilla is the preferred choice. However manzanilla goes well with a broad range of soups, such as chicken or vegetable. It even makes a good partner for that most difficult thing to match, asparagus soup, with its hint of bitterness.

In the seaside resorts of Andalucia, where fish is generally eaten, manzanilla is the universal wine on the table. Its body enables it to accompany even such fully-flavoured fish as dogfish and tuna.

In the south of Spain, the art of frying fish, which is not a simple one, is well appreciated, and there fried fish is one of the most popular seafood dishes. No wine is better suited than manzanilla to accompany this combination of the strong flavours of olive oil and fish. At the mouth of the Guadalquivir, the local fishermen catch a small flat fish like a sole, called *acedia*, which is native to the region and can be eaten freshly fried in the bars of the Bajo de Guía; once again, there is no other accompaniment than manzanilla.

The humble British fish and chips also go well with manzanilla. There are fond memories of ordering some at Aldeburgh on the Suffolk coast and sitting on the sea wall to eat them accompanied by a bottle of manzanilla out of the boot of the car. Whilst the grey waves of the North Sea scarcely resembled those rolling onto a sunlit Atlantic beach, one could almost think one was in Sanlúcar. Such occasions bring back the best gastronomic memories.

Light meats, pâtés and smoked meats, most fish and game go well with manzanilla but it is with ham (particularly from the *pata negra* pig) and charcuterie that it shows its best form in the world of wine-food matching.

Cheese, as long as it is not too mature, goes well with manzanilla and a mild cheddar or half-cured manchego make good partners for it.

Having said all this, there is little doubt that the finest of all marriages is between manzanilla and shellfish. Indeed almost any makes an ideal partner, be it lobster, langoustine, clam, razor clam, barnacle, crab, prawn or mussel. However there are certain that stand out: such a one is the oyster, for the sea water found in its shell goes well with the salty tang of the wine. One idea is to pour a few drops of manzanilla on to the oyster, so as to take in the two typically Sanlúcar flavours at the same time, sea and wine.

There are two other distinctive specialities in Sanlúcar that demand manzanilla: *galeras*, or mantis shrimps, and *ortiguillas*, or sea anenomes. Both these are rarely found elsewhere and are truly delicious.

It is no coincidence that shrimps are the classic dish for manzanilla. Sanlúcar shrimps are of a particular sub-species that thrives at the mouth of the Guadalquivir. They have a distinctive texture and flavour and the marriage of the shellfish's salty flavour and the wine borders on perfection. Shrimps and manzanilla are two of the hallmarks of Sanlúcar; the third is horse-racing on the beach.

Whilst this might be the perfect marriage, manzanilla is capable of many other happy relationships with dishes such as pasta or that typically Spanish dish, *croquetas*.

Indeed there is wide evidence of the wine's gastronomic versatility. The British magazine *Wine* organised a tasting to find the ideal bride for that most intractable of gastronomic partners, asparagus. On parade as suitors was a wide assortment of wines including a Sancerre, a pinot gris from Alsace, a Rueda, Champagne, a muscat and a broad range of sauvignon blancs. It was on the foot of manzanilla that the slipper fitted! Manzanilla sits happily with a broad assortment of vegetables, from beans to artichokes.

At home manzanilla is added to the marinade for all meat stews, whether of beef, lamb or pork. It is also an indispensable ingredient in fish stews and will give you an unforgettable *moules marinières*.

To give you some idea of the versatility of manzanilla, here are some recipes which feature it as an ingredient These come from the book *La Cocina Sanluqueña* by José Carlos García Rodríguez. We offer our thanks to the author for allowing us to reproduce them.

All these recipes are for four persons, unless otherwise stated, and when ripe tomatoes are mentioned, they should be peeled.

PRAWN SOUP
SOPA DE GALERAS

1 kg large prawns in their shells
1 onion, chopped
3 green peppers, sliced
3 ripe tomatoes, sliced
Half a cup of olive oil
A few sprigs of mint
1 small baguette, cut into thin slices
1 glass manzanilla pasada
Salt

Place a casserole dish on the stove with 1 litre of water. Bring to the boil, add the prawns. Reduce the heat, cover the pan and simmer the prawns for 3-6 minutes, depending on the size. Start timing once the water has begun to boil again. The prawns will be cooked when they float to the top and the flesh has turned white or opaque throughout. Cut one in half to check.

Remove the prawns from the heat immediately, drain reserving the cooking water. Run the prawns under cold water for a few seconds to stop the cooking process.

Put the oil, the chopped onion and peppers in a frying pan. Soften them over a low heat and then add the sliced tomatoes. Fry them all together and then put in a blender.

Add the resultant mixture to the stock from the boiled prawns.

Add the salt, mint, bread and the manzanilla pasada.

Boil for some minutes, then add the peeled and chopped prawns.

Serve hot from an earthenware pot.

CLAMS MARINIÈRE
ALMEJAS A LA MARINERA

1 kg clams
3 garlic cloves, chopped
1 small glass of olive oil
1 teaspoon paprika
$\frac{1}{4}$ glass manzanilla
Salt

Brown the chopped garlic in the olive oil in a cast-iron pan.

Wash the clams well and add them and the paprika to the pan.

Sauté them adding the manzanilla and the salt.

Continue doing this over a low flame until all the clams have opened.

DOGFISH MARINIÈRE
CAZÓN A LA MARINERA

1 kg dogfish, sliced
250 g cooked clams, without their shells
150 ml clam stock
½ glass manzanilla
1 kg fried tomato
Salt

Marinade the dogfish in a pot with the clams, the stock and the manzanilla.

Fry the tomatoes in a large pan. When they are just cooked add the dogfish and the other ingredients. Add salt to taste, bring to the boil and simmer for about ten minutes.

DOGFISH AND ONIONS
CAZÓN ENCEBOLLADO

1 kg dogfish, sliced
Parsley, chopped
Nutmeg, few gratings
Olive oil
4 garlic cloves, chopped
Cloves
1 bayleaf
1 kg onions, finely chopped
2 tablespoons flour
1 glass manzanilla
Salt

Place the dogfish in a pot with the chopped parsley and the nutmeg.

Fry up together with a little olive oil the garlic, the cloves, the bay leaf and the onions, thickening the mixture with the flour. Add this and the manzanilla to the fish. Season and simmer until cooked.

SAFFRON DOGFISH
CAZÓN EN AMARILLO

1 kg dogfish, sliced
Virgin olive oil
3 slices bread
4 garlic cloves
Parsley
1 onion
$\frac{1}{2}$ ripe tomato
Pinch saffron
1 glass manzanilla
Salt

Fry the bread and put in a blender with the garlic, a little salt and the parsley. Soften the chopped onion in a pan and add the tomato.

Add the mixture to the blender with the manzanilla, the saffron and a little water.

Place the mixture in a pan and boil for five minutes. Finally add the fish, bring back to the boil and simmer until cooked.

SUMMER VEGETABLE SQUID
CHIPIRONES EN VERANILLO

1 kg squid
2 medium tomatoes
2 green peppers
1 medium onion
4 garlic cloves
1 bay leaf
1 glass manzanilla
1 glass oil

Clean the squid and remove the ink-sacks. Put in a pot with the other ingredients, finely chopped. Cook over a low heat until they are tender, making sure that the sauce binds together.

STEWED CUTTLEFISH
CHOCO GUISADO

1 kg cuttlefish, cleaned and sliced
$\frac{1}{2}$ glass olive oil
1 head of garlic, chopped
1 onion, chopped
3 green peppers, chopped
4 ripe tomatoes, chopped
1 bayleaf
Paprika
1 glass manzanilla
1 glass water
1 pinch saffron
Salt

In a cast-iron pan, soften the garlic, the onion, the peppers, the tomatoes, the bayleaf and the paprika in the olive oil.

Add the cuttlefish, the manzanilla and the water and boil for twenty minutes.

Add the salt and the saffron and let boil for a further couple of minutes.

BAKED DOVER SOLE
LENGUADOS EN TARTERA

2 Dover sole, weight approx 1 kg
Potatoes
Onion
Parsley
Garlic
Bay leaf
Paprika
Breadcrumbs
1 glass manzanilla
Olive oil
Slices of lemon
Salt

Clean the fish and lay them in a baking tin on a bed of very finely sliced potatoes.

In a separate dish chop the remaining ingredients finely and mix with the paprika and the breadcrumbs.

Sprinkle this mixture over the fish and moisten with the manzanilla and the oil.

Place in a hot oven and cook for 20-30 minutes. Serve with the lemon.

BAKED TUNA STEAK
MORRILLO DE ALMADRABA AL HORNO

1 tuna steak (approx 600 g)
Olive oil
1 onion, sliced
2 garlic cloves
Cumin
$\frac{1}{2}$ glass manzanilla
Pepper
Salt
Roast potatoes

Season the tuna and place in a baking dish.

Add a little olive oil, the sliced onion, garlic and the cumin.

Moisten with the manzanilla and cook in a hot oven for about 35 minutes.

Take the fish out when cooked and liquidise the vegetables and juices to make a sauce. Season.

Take the fish off the bone when it has cooled down.

Reheat and serve warm, covered with sauce and garnished with roast potatoes.

SAFFRON MONKFISH
RAPE EN AMARILLO

1 kg monkfish, cut into slices
Olive oil
2 slices bread
5 garlic cloves
Parsley
1 onion, sliced
1 ripe tomato
1 glass manzanilla
Pinch saffron
$^{1}/_{2}$ glass water
Salt

Fry the bread and put it in a blender with the garlic, salt and the parsley. In a pan, gently fry the onion and add the tomato. Then add the blended mixture, the manzanilla, the saffron and the water and reduce. Then add the monkfish and simmer for a further ten minutes.

MONKFISH WITH FRIED BREAD
RAPE AL PAN FRITO

1 kg monkfish, cut into pieces
$^1/_2$ glass olive oil
1 onion, sliced
1 head of garlic, sliced
Parsley
1 red pepper, sliced
1 teaspoon mild paprika
1 glass manzanilla
A little water
4 slices of fried bread
Salt

In a cast-iron pot soften the onion, the garlic and the parsley in the olive oil.

Add the sliced pepper and the paprika.

Stir gently and add the manzanilla, the water and the fried bread.

Put the mixture in a blender, once blended return the mixture to the pan together with the monkfish.

Let it simmer for five to ten minutes until the fish is cooked.

GOOSE IN MANZANILLA SAUCE
ANSAR EN SALSA DE MANZANILLA

Ansar is the Spanish word for a greylag goose; the only
wild goose to be found there.
Serves 6

1 goose
¹/₂ litre olive oil
2 large onions, sliced
10 red peppers, sliced
1 head of garlic, peeled
A handful of parsley
100 g almonds
2 carrots, sliced
1 stick of celery, sliced
2 bay leaves
4 cloves
Black pepper
¹/₂ bottle manzanilla
Salt

Cut the goose into pieces and brown the meat with some of
the oil in a cast-iron pan.

Put the meat on one side and, in the same pan, fry the
sliced onions, the peppers, the garlic and the parsley, then
add the almonds.

Put this mixture in a blender.

Put the goose meat back in the pan, together with the
mixture, the sliced carrots and celery, bay leaves and spices.
Heat up again and add the manzanilla, simmering for a few
minutes. Cover with water and leave to stew until the meat
is cooked and the sauce has reduced. Season with salt and
serve with fried potatoes cut into large cubes.

VEAL IN MANZANILLA SAUCE
CARNE PICANDEAU A LA MANZANILLA

4 x 150 g fillets of veal
1 large onion
1 head of garlic, peeled
Parsley
1 glass olive oil
1 glass manzanilla
Ground pepper
Water

Place the fillets in a casserole and add the onion, the garlic and the parsley chopped very finely.

Moisten with the oil and the manzanilla, season with pepper and cook on a low heat until the meat is tender. If necessary, add a little water as needed, but maintain the consistency of the sauce.

Serve with mashed potatoes.

RABBIT WITH MANZANILLA
CONEJO A LA MANZANILLA

Serves 6

2 kg rabbit, cut up
1 glass olive oil
1 head of garlic, peeled and chopped
1 onion, chopped
Fresh thyme
1 teaspoon mild paprika
100 g fried almonds
2 bay leaves
½ bottle manzanilla
Salt

Sauté the rabbit in a cast-iron pan with the oil and the chopped garlic and onions, thyme, paprika and salt.

Grind the almonds and add them with the bay leaves and the manzanilla to the pan.

Bring to the boil and simmer until tender.

Serve in a clay dish and garnish with fresh thyme.

PACO EL PINO OXTAIL
COLA DE TORO AL ESTILO PACO EL PINO

1 oxtail, cut into pieces
Lard
1 large onion
1 head of garlic
1 sprig parsley
1 tomato
1 red pepper
1 bay leaf
Ground pepper
Nutmeg
Salt
½ bottle manzanilla

Put the pieces of the oxtail in a cast-iron pan and brown in the lard.

Chop the vegetables finely and add to the pan.

Cover with manzanilla and put in a low oven.

Cook slowly so that the sauce thickens and the meat comes away from the bone when served.

MALLARD WITH SUMMER VEGETABLES
PATO AL VERANILLO
Serves 2

1 mallard
Serrano ham
1 glass olive oil
1 onion, sliced
2 garlic cloves, sliced
Parsley
1 glass manzanilla
½ onion, chopped
2 garlic cloves, chopped
Black pepper
Salt

This bird should not be plucked, but rather skinned completely.

Cut it up, splitting it into two and separating the legs.

Rinse well and put in a casserole with the breasts, peppered and larded with the ham.

In another pan, fry the sliced onion and two cloves of garlic, also sliced, and the parsley.

Add this to the duck and sauté well in the original casserole, adding the manzanilla, pepper and salt.

When half-cooked add a further half onion and two cloves of garlic that have been finely chopped.

Braise slowly until the duck becomes tender, adding water if necessary.

When cooked, remove the bird and cut the meat off the bone.

Put the remaining liquid in a blender and cover the duck meat with the sauce.

Serve with mushrooms, rice or mashed potatoes.

VENISON SANLÚCAR-STYLE
VENADO A LA SANLUQUEÑA

750 g venison
1 glass olive oil
6 garlic cloves, sliced
2 large onions, sliced
4 carrots, sliced
Black pepper
1 glass manzanilla pasada
Water
Salt

Cut up the meat and sauté it in the oil in a casserole.

Add the sliced garlic and onions, sliced carrots, salt and pepper and manzanilla pasada. Bring to the boil and then reduce the heat. Cook slowly until the meat is tender, adding water if necessary.

Manzanilla and Wine Tourism

We live in a time when we like to see what is ahead of us. We want to plan so that, both in our work and in our leisure time, we can prepare for our future. As far as the wine trade in Sanlúcar is concerned, not without our difficulties, we are weathering the storm, brought on by increased competition in the market. This has led to enhanced sales of manzanilla, particularly in Spain over the past few years.

The same can be said of local tourism. We have held our own at a time of increased competition, particularly in the field of prices, and when tourists are seeking different places to visit. What Sanlúcar can offer is sun and beaches, great food and hospitality.

Nevertheless, we are having to adapt what we offer to

meet the demands of the market, by giving greater choice and by trying to match supply to demand. It is here that oenotourism should come into its own, bringing both sectors together, to offer Sanlúcar, without the need of great capital expenditure, as the ideal destination. Here we must profit from the worldwide reputation of our wines. With this in mind, promotional films have recently been made. Also there has been created, with the support of the Sanlúcar town council and various local companies, the Ruta del Vino y Brandy del Marco de Jerez. This plan should help stress how important Sanlúcar is for manzanilla, and how important manzanilla is for Sanlúcar.

In the wine world, we have a long and proud history. This dates back to the Phoenicians, seven centuries before Christ, when, it has been claimed, grapes were first grown here to be made into wine. We can state with pride that we have a wine tradition of almost three millennia.

We are fortunate in where we find ourselves. Here two great continents, Africa and Europe and two great seas, the Atlantic and the Mediterranean, meet. This has meant that we have been the point through which each succeeding civilisation has had to expand. Each of these civilisations has left its traces. Here are fused together the cultures of the Greeks, the Romans and the Arabs. We have offered them an open field in which they have sowed their seeds.

Despite our having spent five hundred years under Arab domination and, despite their having prohibited the consumption of alcohol, our vintners have continued with their work, overcoming all problems and developing the industry. Indeed, it is the Arabs who brought to us from China the art of distillation. Without this, our important trade in brandy would not exist, and we would not be able to produce fortified wines. They also introduced us to the raisin, which opened the way to our making sweet wines.

With the expulsion of the Arabs, by Alfonso the Wise, also known as the 'winemaker king', the area under vines increased considerably when he granted lands to the nobles who had supported him. These he obliged to plant and maintain vineyards. With the age of exploration, the Sanlúcar wine trade flourished as this was the departure point for many voyages of discovery, and for those for supplying the newly created colonies. The reputation of our wines thus spread rapidly around the expanding known world.

This commerce led to wine merchants from all over Europe coming to establish themselves in Sanlúcar, particularly during the eighteenth century. They came from the United Kingdom, Germany, Holland, Ireland, France, the north of Spain, particularly Cantabria, Castilla-Leon and other parts of Andalucia. With the passing of time, these outsiders married into local families, and thus were created many of today's sherry houses, some of which have been in the same family for seven generations or more. It is not surprising that the major markets for our wines became those from where these families had come.

At one stage many former church buildings were used as warehouses, but increased trade meant the construction of further bodegas and they now form an important part of our wine heritage; an irresistible attraction for the wine tourist.

Hospitality in these cellars is an old tradition as writers such as Ford and Vizetelly have noted. Indeed, individual companies have considered their welcome to be an essential part of their marketing strategy, introducing potential customers to their wines and sealing their fidelity with numerous *cañas* of manzanilla.

Hospitality centres in the various bodegas featured in the Ruta del Vino now welcome more than 600,000 visitors each year. For many of these tourists it is their first introduction to wine culture in all its forms, be it architecture, tools of the trade or the end product. This culture has come together through our history, our soil, our climate, our food and, most important of all, our wines.

It is our geographical situation that makes the sherry region unique. To the north are the marshes and the mouth of the Guadalquivir, which casts its influence on the limestone soils of Lebrija and Trebujena, before coming to the ocean with Sanlúcar on the left bank and the Coto Doñana on the right. Just along the Atlantic coast is the town of Chipiona. This Atlantic is our western frontier and, together with the salt-pans of the Bay of Cádiz, dominates the life of the towns of Rota, Puerto Real, Chiclana and El Puerto de Santa Maria, where the Guadalete river reaches the sea, having flowed through many of the Jerez vineyards. We have here a triangle bounded by water, which is familiar to those tourists who come to enjoy the beaches, but perhaps less well-known by wine-tourists, who can enjoy it all year around.

To travel amongst these green, leafy vineyards, planted with palomino, pedro ximenez and muscatel grapes, can be just as rewarding as visiting the bodegas filled with wines and brandies, ageing in butts of American oak, where life first begins for manzanilla and other wines, initially under its veil of flor and then through the various criaderas to the ultimate solera.

Do not think that it is just wines and brandies in Sanlúcar and the region around it. Here, within the Ruta del Vino have been brought together a broad range of attractions. To our rich historic inheritance of castles, citadels, cathedrals, churches and monasteries, can be added specialised museums, national parks and nature reserves, the Royal Andalucian School of Equestrian Arts, herds of horses and iconic expressions of our land such as the flamenco and the fairs and pilgrimages.

Added to all this is the regional gastronomy, with wine as an essential ingredient for so many recipes and as the ideal partner for our dishes. Our gardens, our animals and our sea offer up their riches to our chefs, so that they can create both traditional dishes as well as modern interpretations of their art. In the sherry region, there is breadth and depth in the range of restaurants and a wide range of prices. Wherever you go, however, quality, service and value are always evident. Just as there is variety in the dishes, so there is in the range of wines. Every palate that comes to visit us will go away satisfied.

Hospitality is a key word in Sanlúcar and this is reflected in the range of hotels on offer, again with a variety of styles and prices. Here hospitality and professionalism go hand in hand to make a stay in Sanlúcar, with all its many attractions, unforgettable. Autumn and winter are the best seasons in which to visit Sanlúcar, to discover what is at its heart, all that goes to make it: the style of life of the sanluqueño, the quality of life within the town and the warmth of the people there.

Manzanilla – Its Future in the World of Wine

From its appearance at the end of the eighteenth century and the beginning of the nineteenth, manzanilla has conquered the local market and has a vital part to play in the customs and traditions of Andalucia – the Seville fair first took place in 1847 – but it has scarcely scratched the surface of the wine market in other parts of Spain and elsewhere in the world. Until the 90s, it accounted for no more than 8.5% of the sales of sherry. Its distribution was mainly in the hands of merchants who had come to the region, from the mountains of northern Spain as a result of the encouragement given by Carlos III. On the other hand, the merchants in Jerez were largely foreigners, predominantly

British. From as early as 1700, this helped them to sell their wines widely in the world. The Empire was their captive market. In contrast, manzanilla remained firmly where it was born, Andalucia. While foreign merchants produced wines with varying degrees of sweetness, which made them more appealing to their customers. manzanilla remained faithful to its original conception, light and bone-dry. It seems that when the manzanilla producers offered their wines to potential customers abroad, they failed to persuade them as to the ideal way they should be drunk; that is, just as they are drunk in the south of Spain.

The result is that in foreign markets manzanilla is considered solely as an aperitif, whilst in Andalucia, it is drunk throughout the meal, which naturally leads to an increase in per capita consumption! All this goes to show that being the most individual and exclusive wine in the group to which it belongs, has restricted its export possibilities.

Antoine Latour, in the nineteenth century, stated that, "No wine could be vulgar which has its special glass". As has already been mentioned, the special glass of manzanilla is the *caña*, which is almost cylindrical in shape and with vertical indentations, called *balcones*. It even has its own form of tray, a *cañero*, like an old-fashioned two-tiered cake stand, with holes in the upper level into which you insert the glasses. This gives them more stability on the occasions when they are traditionally used, such as at fairs and on pilgrimages, when the consumer might well be on horseback. The humble background to manzanilla's image is suggested by Fernando Sabater, in his book *A caballo entre dos Milenios*, when he says of the wine that since the past century "it plays a role amongst the fortified wines of Andalucia, similar to that of Beaujolais in the French wine ranks".

Why, then, is manzanilla the 'great unknown' in foreign markets?

One reason is that not enough effort has been placed on its promotion. Secondly, it has failed to create around itself the image of the important role that it plays in everyday life in southern Spain – why it has become the everyday drink of the people.

Here we have the driest, most delicate and most exclusive wine in its class of fortified wines. In addition to this manzanilla has two outstanding characteristics. Firstly, it has the most powerful of aromas, which immediately become apparent to all those in the room when a cork is drawn. Moreover, this aroma is fragrant and penetrating, as complex as that given by a bunch of flowers: fresh and totally natural.

On top of all this, it is one of the most organic and ecological wines, being created without the aid of chemicals and additives. For its existence it relies on a totally natural biological agent – flor – which produces oxygen and thus improves the atmosphere. Each bodega could be described as an integrated nature reserve containing hundreds of other smaller reserves – the butts – the presence of which within the town of Sanlúcar help purify the ambient air.

Nevertheless, manzanilla, and all dry sherries, are not easy wines to sell, for the initial reaction of someone who tastes them for the first time is almost always one of displeasure. On the other hand, if the first taste takes place in a bodega or a quayside bar in the Bajo de Guía, the reaction is almost inevitably one of approval. It is the difference between eating a freshly picked tomato and one that has been picked green and artificially ripened, before arriving on the supermarket shelves.

What the producers must do is to educate the consumer

as to how manzanilla is drunk in its homeland. At social evenings in Andalucia, it is manzanilla that encourages conversation. It will be accompanied by olives, potato crisps, dried fruit and whatever. At flamenco parties, it will always be partnered by a broad range of tapas, including small portions of all sorts of dishes, which might range from *salmorejo*, a type of thick, cold soup, to shrimp omelette, just to show you the potential breadth of the choice. In a restaurant, manzanilla will regularly accompany the entrée and will almost certainly be drunk with seafood.

Such education of potential consumers does not come cheap, and, as has been said already, only three companies have been prepared to back such a campaign in the British market. The programme of education came in three stages: firstly through the specialist press, both in the wine trade and in gastronomy; secondly through the wine trade itself and finally the consumer. Amongst the events were tastings of different wines with different oysters; complete menus around manzanilla and visits by journalists and customers to Sanlúcar, its vineyards and its bodegas. These last took place around local celebrations when the wine would be drunk most openly! The results exceeded expectations: during the first year of the campaign, more than half all mentions of sherry in the press were about manzanilla, and all the participating bodegas saw a dramatic increase in their sales. Restaurant owners, sommeliers and wine writers have all been enthused by the inherent quality and appeal of the wines and it is to be hoped that they, in their turn will be able to enthuse their customers and their readers. All this has managed to break down certain pre-conceptions about sherry and to set manzanilla apart as a wine with individuality, a wine with a character of is own.

Such promotions should continue; backed up by some

basic suggestions.

For example, manzanilla should be served chilled. This is a relative term and must depend on the local temperature. For example, a summer picnic on the Long Mynd in Shropshire requires its wine to be at a different temperature to that for a picnic on the beach in Sanlúcar in August.

Another suggestion is that it should be served in its traditional glass, the caña, or, failing that in a sherry copita, whose shape prevents contact with the hand warming up the wine. On the other hand, when drunk at home, it can be served in a full-size white wine glass. Manzanilla is a fine wine and should be treated as such, by being a glass that is worthy of its status,

Manzanilla is a wine not to be hurried; each mouthful should be savoured. Finally, it is important to study the label on the bottle, to confirm that it is a genuine manzanilla de Sanlúcar de Barrameda. And so you can recognise again those wines you have enjoyed.

Whatever promotional efforts are made in the future for manzanilla, it seems likely that it will never become a wine of mass consumption, but rather a niche item for the true specialist and connoisseur. Within Spain, it seems certain that it will continue its role as the essential wine for certain occasions. In foreign markets, it should enjoy a similar place to that of quality port, always drunk on special occasions. Moreover, the top brands that spend money on promotion and publicity will be the ones that benefit, exploiting to the full the exclusivity, the individuality and the quality that all go to make the wine that is manzanilla.

Glossary

Abocado: **Sp**. Medium-sweet,

Acedia: **Sp**. A small flatfish of the sole family, found at the mouth of the Guadalquivir.

Albariza: **Sp**. The chalky soil on which the best sherry grapes are grown.

Almacenista: **Sp**. lit: a warehousekeeper. A wholesaler. In the sherry region, one who ages wines and then sells it in bulk.

Amontillado: **Sp**. lit: something that has taken on the characteristics of a montilla wine. An aged fino sherry, which has softened and filled out.

Aranzada: **Sp**. An historic measurement of area, approximately equivalent to an acre.

Arena: **Sp**. Sand. The poorest soil of the sherry vineyards, often used for growing moscatel grapes.

Arroba: **Sp**. An historic liquid measurement equal to 25 litres.

Artesanía absoluta: **Sp**. Total craftmanship.

Bajeta: **Sp**. The base on which the barrels are ranged in the warehouse.

Balcón: **Sp**. Balcony.

Barro: **Sp**. Clay; inferior soils for the production of sherry.

Blanco: **Sp**. White.

Bodega: **Sp**. A warehouse for storing wine. It can also be a place where wine is sold or the hold of a ship.

Bota: **Sp**. A butt (q.v.) or a boot.

Butt: Eng. The traditional cask for the storing and shipment of sherry of 108 imp. gallons. Made of American oak.

Campo: **Sp**. A field that is ploughed; thus it can be a vineyard. The countryside.

Caña: **Sp**. *1*. A special small tumbler that is traditionally used for drinking manzanilla. *2*. The instrument used for withdrawing wine through the bunghole in Sanlúcar bodegas, as opposed to the venencia (q.v.) of Jerez. Normally made of bamboo.

Cañero: **Sp**. A special tray for carrying the cañas, manzanilla glasses.

Clase: **Sp**. A single stage in the criadera (q.v.) system of ageing sherries.

Copita: **Sp**: A tulip-shaped glass, traditionally used for drinking sherry.

Corrales: **Sp**: Depressions in the sand dunes, sheltered from the wind. It is here that, in Sanlúcar, one finds the vine nurseries.

Criadera: **Sp**. lit. a nursery. A stage in the fractional bending system that is used in the production of sherry. The final criadera is the solera (q.v.).

Croqueta: **Sp**. A croquette or rissole.

Denominación de Origen, D.O.: **Sp**. lit. Denomination of Origin. An official classification of Spanish quality wine; the equivalent of the French *appellation contrôlée*.

Dulce: **Sp**. Sweet.

Fería: **Sp**. A Fair. This can either be a commercial fair or a local celebration that takes place over a number of days in most Spanish towns and villages, often around the local saint's day. That of

Seville is one of the most noteworthy.

Fino: **Sp**. One of the two basic styles of sherry (the other being oloroso). It is influenced by flor (q.v.) and is the base wine for all manzanillas.

Flor: **Sp**. lit. flower. A range of fungi of the *saccharomyces* family, which grows on the surface of fino sherries (and certain other wines in Spain and elsewhere) and prevents oxidation. In Sanlúcar, it is present all the year round, whereas in other parts of the sherry region it varies seasonally.

Galera: **Sp**. The mantis shrimp, a speciality of Sanlúcar.

Gitana: **Sp**. A gypsy woman. Gitano is a male gypsy.

Guita: **Sp**. Either a cord or a slang word for cash.

Jarra: **Sp**. A pitcher, a large jug that was, in former times, used by cellarmen to transfer wine from one cask to another.

Malleto: **Sp**. lit. A heavy hammer traditionally used for beating paper pulp, but locally in Sanlúcar, a small vineyard owner, who makes his living from growing grapes.

Manzanilla fina: **Sp**. The fresher style of manzanilla that passes through a lesser number of clases (q.v.). This is now the fashionable style.

Manzanilla Pasada: **Sp**. A more mature style of manzanilla, that, traditionally, was the preferred style.

Moscatel: **Sp**. A lesser grape variety grown in the sherry region for making sweet wines. It is generally grown on sandy soils.

Mosto: **Sp**. This can either mean must (unfermented grape-juice), or fermented wine before it is aged in cask. In Sanlúcar, it generally appears to mean the latter.

Must: Eng. Unfermented grape juice.

Navaza: **Sp**. A corral (q.v.) close to the town, planted either with vegetables or young vines.

Négociant: **Fr**. In the wine trade, someone who buys wine or grapes from the grower and then markets it under his own name.

Oloroso: **Sp**. lit. fragrant. A full-bodied style of sherry that has not been iinfluenced by flor (q.v.).

Ortiquilla: **Sp**. A sea anenome – when deep-fried, is a local delicacy in Sanlúcar.

Pago: **Sp**. A planted area of land, more particularly in the sherry region, one planted with vines. One pago may well include a number of different campos, or individual vineyards.

Pajarete: **Sp**. A rich, deeply-coloured wine, used for adding colour and sweetness to sherries. It takes its name from a monastery near Jerez.

Palomino: **Sp**. The main grape used in the production of sherry – and a number of other wines. It is also a table grape.

Pata Negra: **Sp**. lit. black hoof. A Spanish breed of pigs that is renowned for the quality of hams that they give.

Pedro Ximénez: **Sp**. The main grape of Montilla. For sherry, it is used for making sweet wines. Legend has it that it is the riesling grape, brought from Germany by a sailor called Peter Siemens. An alternative story has it that he was a soldier sent to fight in the Low Countries, at the time of Carlos V.

Phylloxera: **Lat**. A pest which came over from America in the nineteenth century and destroyed most of the vineyards in Europe. It is still present in the vineyards of the world. The most effective solution, so far, has been to graft European vines on to American rootstock.

Rama: **Sp**. Lit. branch. En rama: a style of manzanilla that is bottled straight from the cask, without filtration and treatment.

Real: **Sp** Lit. royal. A historic silver coin, with varying values in Spain and the Americas.

Rociado: lit. bedewed. The refilling of casks in the solera system.

el Rocío: A shrine in the Doñana, to which there is a pilgrimage, from all over Andalucia, each year at Pentecost.

Ruta del Vino: **Sp**. Wine road.

Saca: **Sp**. Lit. withdrawal. The act of taking wine from one criadera to the next.

Sanluqueño: **Sp**. The adjective from Sanlúcar. A native of that town.

Seco: **Sp**. Dry.

Solera: **Sp**. In the production of sherry, the final clase (q.v.) from which the wine is drawn off for blending and bottling.

Tapa: **Sp**. A snack, and a good excuse for drinking manzanilla.

Tercio de frutos: **Sp**. Lit. a third of the fruits. A tax imposed on cargoes, normally 10 per cent of their value.

Tinaja: **Sp**. A large earthenware vessel, in the shape of an Ali-Baba basket, used for the fermentation and storage of wine, now replaced amost universally by stainless steel, but still found in Montilla and certain other Spanish wine regions.

Tinto: **Sp**. (of wine) red.

Tío: **Sp**. Uncle.

Venencia: **Sp**. An instrument used in Jerez, for drawing off samples of wine through the bung hole, with a silver cylindrical cup at the end of a long flexible handle, which was traditionally made of whalebone, but now, more generally of fibreglaas. (The equivalent tool in a Sanlúcar cellar is a caña q.v.) The man who uses a venencia is a venenciador.

Venta: **Sp** An roadside bar or restaurant, which might, or might not, also offer accommodation.

Vin de Pays: **Fr**. Lit. wine of the country. In the French wine hierarchy, one step up from *vin de table*. The Spanish equivalent is *vino de la tierra*.

Vino de color: **Sp**. Colour wine, used for darkening sherries.

Vino generoso: **Sp**. Fortified wine.

Bibliography

Allen, David Rayvern, (ed.) *Arlott on Wine*, Willow Books, London 1992.

Allen, H. Warner, *Sherry*, Constable & Co. Ltd., London 1933.

Barbadillo Delgado, Pedro, *Historia de la Ciudad de Sanlúcar de Barrameda*. Ed. Escelicer, Cádiz, 1942.

Barbadillo Rodriguez, Manuel. *La Ejecutorio de la Manzanilla*. Antonio Barbadillo, Jerez 1984

   -      -   *La Manzanilla*, Antonio Barbadillo, Sanlúcar de Barrameda, 1995

Barry, Sir Edward, *Observations Historical, Critical and Medical on the Wines of the Ancients*, T.Cadell, London, 1775.

Borrego Plá, María del Carmen, *El Jerez, Hacedor de Cultura*. Vol 1 (1998) and 2 (2003) Caja San Fernando y Consejo Regulador de las DDOO Jerez, Manzanilla Vinagre, Jerez de la Frontera.

Boutelou, Esteban. *Idea de la Práctica Enológica de Sanlúcar de Barrameda*. Antonio Barbadillo, Sanlúcar de Barrameda 1991.

   -      -   *Memoria sobre el Cultivo de la Vid en Sanlúcar de Barrameda y Xerez de la Frontera*. Imprenta de Villapando, Madrid 1807.

Butler, Frank Hedges, *Wine and the Wine Lands of the World*. T. Fisher Unwin, London, 1916.

Chapman, Abel, *Memories of Fourscore Years Less Two*. Gurney and

Jackson, London, 1930.

Croft-Cooke, Rupert. *Sherry*. Putman, London 1955.

Cuevas, José and Jesús de las. *Vida y Milagros del Vino de Jerez*. Sexta S.A., Jerez de la Frontera 1979

Denman, James L. *What should we Drink?*, Longmans & Co., London 1868.

- - *The Vine and its Fruit*, Longmans, Green & Co., London 1875.

Duijker, Hubrecht. *The Wine Atlas of Spain*, Mitchell Beazley, London 1992.

Ford, Richard. *Gatherings from Spain*. J.M.Dent, London 1906

Fifield, William. *The Sherry Royalty*, Sexta S.A., Jerez de la Frontera 1978.

García del Barrio Ambrosy, Isidro, *La Tierra del Vino de Jerez*, Sexta S.A., Jerez de la Frontera, 1979.

- - - - , *Las Bodegas del Vino de Jerez*. Booklet INIA no. 16 MAPA 1984.

García Rodriguez, José Carlos, *Vinos Andaluces*, Algaida Editores, Seville 1990.

- - - - , *Las Carreras de Caballos de Sanlúcar de Barrameda*, La Sociedad de Carreras de Caballos de Sanlúcar de Barrameda, Sanlúcar de Barrameda 1995.

- - - - , *La Cocina Sanluqueña y sus Mejores Recetas*, Ed. Pequeñas Ideas, Sanlúcar de Barrameda 2000.

Gómez Díaz, Ana María, *La Manzanilla, Historia y Cultura de las Bodegas de Sanlúcar*, Ed. Pequeñas Ideas, Sanlúcar de Barrameda, 2002.

González Gordon, Manuel María, *Jerez-Xérès-Sherry*. The author, Jerez de la Frontera, 1948.

- - - - , *Sherry*, Cassell, London 1972.

- - - - , *Sherry*, The Cookery Book Club, London, 1972.

Healy, Maurice, *Stay Me with Flagons*, Michael Joseph, London, 1954.

Henderson, Dr. A. *The History of Ancient and Modern Wines*, Baldwin Cradock & Joy, London 1824.

Hidalgo, Javier, *Recuerdos de la Marisma*, Ed.Geribel, 2005.

Jeffs, Julian, *Sherry*, Faber & Faber, London 1970.

Latour, Antoine, *La Baie de Cadix*, Michel Lévy Frères, Paris, 1858.

Los Vinos de Jerez, Consejo Regulador, Jerez de la Fronters.n.d..

Layton T.A., *Wines and Castles of Spain*. White Lion, London 1971.

Maldonado Rosso, Javier (ed.), *Las Rutas del Vino en Andalucia*, Fundación José Manuel Lara, Seville, 2006.

M'Bride, D. *General Instruction for the Choice of Wine and Spirituous Liquors*, J.Richardson, London , 1793.

Morewood, Samuel *Philosophical and Statistical History of the Inventions and Customs of Ancient and Modern Nations in the Manufacture and Use of Inebriating Liquors*, William Curry Jnr. & Co. and William Carson, Dublin, 1838.

Mountford, Guy, *Portrait of a Wilderness, the Story of the Coto Doñana Expeditions*, Hutchinson, London, 1958.

Peñín, José ed., *Guia Peñín de los Vinos de España 2009*, Peñín Ediciones, Madrid 2008.

Redding, Cyrus, *A History and Description of Modern Wines*, Henry G. Bohn, London, 1851.

Saintsbury, George, *Notes on a Cellar Book*, Macmillan and Co., London 1920.

Savater, Fernando, *A Caballo Entre Milenios*, Ed. Aguilar, Madrid 2001.

Shannon, Dr R. *A Practical Treatise on Brewing, Distilling and Rectification....*, R. Scholey, London 1805.

Shaw, Thomas George, *Wine, the Vine and the Cellar*, Longman, Roberts and Green, London, 1864.

Terrington, William. *Cooling Cups and Dainty Drinks*. George Routledge and Sons, London, 1870.

Thudicum, Dr. J.L.W., *The Lancet Report on Sherry*, George Bell and Sons, London, 1896.

-     -   - and Dupré, Dr. August, *A Treatise on the Origin, Nature and Varieties of Wine*, Macmillan & Co. Ltd., London 1872.

Verdad, Don Pedro (pseudo.), *From Vineyard to Decanter*, Edward Stanford, London, 3rd ed. 1876

Vizetelly, Henry, *The Wines of the World*, Ward, Lock and Tyler, London 1875.

-     - , *Facts about Sherry*, Ward, LLock and Tyler, London, 1876.

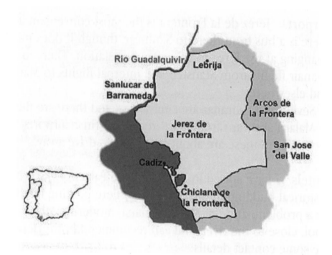

Hints for the Visitor

A word of warning, Sanlúcar is not just a wine town, but also a popular holiday resort, so the hotels tend be booked well in advance for the months of July and August.

Websites: There are two websites which are full of useful information, particularly about feasts and festivities, in addition to accommodation. These are the local www.sanlúcar-de-barrameda.com and the more regional www.rutadeljerezbrandy.es.

Airports: Jerez de la Frontera is the most convenient and there is a bus from there to Sanlúcar, though it does mean changing at the Jerez town-centre bus station. There are Ryanair flights from Stansted and internal flights to Madrid and elsewhere.

Seville and Gibraltar are alternatives and there are flights to Malaga and Faro from many regional British airports, though both these are about three hours' drive away.

Hotels: I have stayed in the Posada de Palacio, which is a historical building in the old town, where parking might be a problem, and the Maciá Doñana, modern, with a pool, close to the river, and can recommend both. Here are some contact details:

Maciá Doñana: *tel*: (0034) 956 365 000
www.maciahoteles.com
Posada del Palacio: *tel*: (0034) 956 365 840
www.posadadelpalacio.com
Palacio Ducal de Medina Sidonia: *tel*: (0034) 956 360 161
www.ruralduquesmedina.sidonia.com
Los Helechos: *tel*: (0034) 956 361 349
www.hotelloshelechos.com
Barrameda: *tel*: (0034) 956 385 878
www.hotel.barrameda.com

Restaurants and bars: There are two main centres for these at Bajo de Guía, along the riverside quay, looking over to the Coto Doñana, and on Plaza Cabildo in the town centre. At the first is Casa Bigote, a tapas bar with an international reputation and, across the alleyway that runs alongside it, the restaurant of the same name. Just along the street is the Mirador Doñana restaurant. At the second are two excellent bars Balbino and La Gitana. Both have speciality tapas. Other addresses to look out for are La Lonja, Joselito Huertas and El Poma.

You will notice that the locals do not order their sherry by the glass, but rather by the half-bottle.

Bodega visits: Most bodegas welcome visitors, but some of them are better geared up to receive them, with dedicated staff, whilst others need to have prior notice. It is generally better to book your visit in advance. Here are the contact details:

Bodega Barbadillo: Luis de Eguilaz 11, Sanlúcar. *Tel*: 956 385 201 *e-mail*: barbadillo@barbadillo.com *web*: www.barbadillo.com

Bodegas CAYDSA: Puerto 21, Sanlúcar. *Tel*: 956 361 491 *e-mail*: covica@intrbook.net

Bodegas Delgado Zuleta: Sanlúcar-Chipiona road 1.5km., Sanlúcar. *Tel*: 956 360 543 *e-mail*: exportacion@delgadozuleta.com *web*: www.delgadozuleta.com

Bodegas Herederos de Argüeso: Mar 8, Sanlúcar. *Tel*: 956 385 116 *web*: www.argueso.es

Bodegas Hidalgo La Gitana: Banda Playa 42, Sanlúcar. *Tel*: 956 385 304 *e-mail*: bodegashidalgo@lagitana.es *web*: www.lagitana.es

Bodegas La Cigarrera: Torno, Sanlúcar. *Tel*: 956 381 285
e-mail: lacigarrera@bodegaslacigarrera.com
web: www.bodegaslacigarrera.com

Bodegas La Guita: Sanlúcar-Jerez road 1km, Misericordia
1, Sanlúcar. *Tel*: 956 319 564 *e-mail*:
laguita@laguita.com
web: www.laguita.com

Bodegas Pedro Romero: Transbolsa 84, Sanlúcar.
Tel: 956 360 736 *e-mail*: pedroromero@pedroromero.es
web: www.pedroromero.es

Bodega de los Angeles: This does not appear in the
main body of the book as it is mainly a venue for weddings and banquets. It does, however, carry on a second-
ary role as an almacenista, with 800 butts.
Luis de Eguilaz 12, Sanlúcar. *Tel*: 956 385 201
e-mail: aurora@yuste.com
web: www.celebracioneslosangeles.com

Index

A.

Ahold Group, Holland 75, 111

Albariza soil 47, 48, 73

Alegría, manzanilla brand 111

Almacenistas 21, 67, **101-104**

Amontillado 34, 52.

Arenas soil 47

Argüeso, Herederos de, company 19, 42, 55, 58, **68-70**, 78

Argüeso, Pape 116

Arlott, John 33,34

Asher, Gerald 95

Aurora, manzanilla brand 98

B.

Bajo de Guía, quarter of Sanlúcar 22, 24. 63, 116, 143., manzanilla brand 79

Balbaina pago 91, 100, 110

Barbadillo, Antonio, company 19, 42, 43 56, **70-76**, 78, 94

Barbadillo, Antonio 74

Barbadillo, Benigno 71-72

Barbadillo family 8, 71

Barbadillo Rodríguez, Manuel 32, 38-40

Baron, Bodegas, company 19, 69, **76-77**

Barros soil 47

Boutelou, Claudio 36

Boutelou, Esteban 36-37

Bodegas: Arboledilla 56, 76. de los Molinillos 77 San Luis 56 construction of: 55-58

Bodegas Unidas S.A., company 78

Busby, James 41

Butt, sherry cask 54, 59

C.

Caballero sherry group 13, 109

Cádiz 11, 40, 41

Caña, glass 27,55 cellar implement 55

Carlos III of Spain 28

Carp, Dutch wine family 94

Castillo del Espiritu Santo 28

Castillo de San Diego, wine brand 43, 75

C.A.Y.D.S.A., company **77-79**

Chapman, Abel 25, 30

La Cigarrera, company 19, **79-80**

Clase 50

Columbus 13, 35

Co-operative cellars 67 del Campo Virgen de la Caridad 78 del Campo de Viticultores de Sanlúcar 80

Corrales 29

Coto Doñana, national park 23, **25-39**, 75

Covisan, sherry company **80-81**

Criaderas 50, 51, 52, 53,58

Croft Original, sherry brand 20, 108

Cuevas Jurado, Manuel, almacenista 103, 109-110

D.

Damaso, Manuel García de Velasco, company 40

Delgado Zuleta, Company 19, 41, **81-83**

Derby, Earl of 18

Dry Sack, sherry brand 111

E.

Elcano, Juan Sebastian 13

English consuls to Sanlúcar 13, 14

Estevez, José, wine group 96

F.

F.W.C. (F.W.Cozens) 12

Fería de Manzanilla 23

Fería de Sevilla 62, 114, 141

J.Ferris M., company **83**

Fino sherries 34, 42, 50, 52, 61
Flor 19, 49 52, 53 58
Florido, Gaspar, company (Florido Hermanos) 19, 46, **83-85**, 99
Ford, Richard 16, 37, 110

G.
García de Barrio Ambrosy, Isidro 44, 56
Garvey, sherry company 20
Gil de Ledesma Sotomayor, Francisco, company 41
Gil Luque M. company 96
La Gitana, manzanilla brand 21, 54, 90-91
Godoy, Manuel de 15, 36, 39, 40
Gomez, Ana María 19
Gonzalez Byass, company, 20, 22 42, 102, **105-109**
Gonzalez del Castillo, Juan Ignacio 40
Gonzalez Gordon, Manuel M. 15, 44, 49, 58, 62
La Goya, manzanilla brand 81, 82
Grape varieties 48
Guadalquivir river 10, 15, 23, 26, 28, 116
La Guita, manzanilla brand 22, 54, 89, 94-97

Gutierrez de Aguera, José, company 41

H.
Harvey's Bristol Cream, sherry brand 20-21,42, 73-74
Henry VIII of England 13
Hidalgo, Emilio, sherry company 89
Hidalgo, Javier 75, 91-92
Hidalgo-La Gitana, company 19, 42 76, 78, **85-92**, 108
Hidalgo Verjano, Eduardo 86
El Hornillo, pago 100
Horse races at Sanlúcar 23, 27
Huelva, wiines of 37-39

I.
Infantes de Orleáns-Borbón, company **92-94**
International Distillers and Vintners 28

J.
James, Walter 36

L.
Lacave, Rodríguez, company 81
Layton, Tommy 38
Listan, grape variety 36-37
Lustau, Emilio, company 103, **108-110**

M.
M'Bride D. 16
Magellan 13, 35
Majon, Viuda de R., company 107

Manzanilla 16, 18, 20, 21-24, 27, 31 32, 34-43 – amontillado 34 – fina 22, 34 – olorosa 107 – pasada 22, 34
origins of name 34-41
production of 44ff
relationship to sherry 60ff vineyards 44-45
Manzanilla, town of Huelva province 37-40
Maria Luisa, Queen of Spain 36
Martelilla, pago 100
Las Medallas, manzanilla brand 69
Medina Group 75, 111, 112
Medina-Sidonia, Duchess of 8, 38
Medina-Sidonia, Dukes of 12, 13, 14, 26, 38-39
Mendez, Bodegas 99
Merchant Venturers of Seville 15
Miraflores pago 44, 46,88, 91, 96
Merimée, Prosper 18
Monpensier family: 45, 86, 92-94, 111
Moscatel grape 48
Mountford, Guy 30

N.
Napoleon 18, 28 sherries 86-87
Navazos 29

O.
Oloroso sherry 34, 50
Ostrych, William 13
Otaolaurruchi, company 21

P.
Paez Luis, company 111, 112
Palomino grape 37-38 48-49
Papirusa, manzanilla brand 110
Pastrana, vineyard 46, 91
Pedro Ximénez grape 48, 60
Perez Megia, Hijos de, company 21, 111, 112
Phylloxera 19, 47
Puerto de Santa María 15
Punto Azul brandy 97

R.
Rainera Perez, Hijos de, company 89, **94-97**
En Rama sherry 75
El Rocio, pilgrimage 23, 31, 109, 115 hamlet 31 manzanilla brand 42, 104, 108
Rockwater sherry 18
Rodríguez, Pedro 72

Romero, Pedro, company **97-99**
Ruiz-Mateos, Zoilo 20-21, 22, 73, 111
Rumasa Group 22, 73-74, 76, 96, 111
Nueva Rumasa 79
Ruta del Vino 137, 139

S.
Sabater, Fernando 142
Sainz de Baranda, Bodegas 100
Salt pans 28-29, 88, 106
Sanchez Ayala, Miguel, company 100
San León, manzanilla brand 47, 58, 70
Sanlúcar de Barrameda 10-18, 22-24, 25, 31, 32 vineyards of 44-45 66-67 wines of 16, 19
San Patricio, sherry brand 20
Santana, Alberto Ramos 40
Serra, Carlos, brand 99
Seville fería 62, 114, 141
Shannon Dr. R. 16
Shaw T.G. 87
Soils 47-48
Solear, manzanilla brand 42
Solera system 19, 50-51 52-52, 54, 58ff

T.
Tapas, origin of 115

Tercio de frutas 15
Tio Pepe, sherry brand 20, 22-23, 42, 105-106
Toledo J.A., letter from 17
Torrebreva vineyard 44, 45-46, 93, 106V.
Vineyards: Pagos:
  Balbaina 91, 100, 110 el Hornillo 100 Miraflores 44, 46, 88, 91, 96
Campos: La
  Callejuelas 110 la Cruz de Husillo 110 Finca Atalaya 77 Finca Martin Miguel 77 la Pastrana 46, 91 Poedo 69,77 Torrebreva 44, 45-46, 93, 106 Viña el Alamo, 88, 98 Viña Armijo 48, 84
Viña el Cuadrado 88, 91 Viña Dolores Nudi 82 Viña Santa Lucia 75
Vizetelly, Henry: 45, 72, 87, 93, 95, 107

W.
Williams & Humbert, company 74-75 110-112

Z.
Zalema, Huelva grape variety 38